I0820330

Leadership and the Sin of Empathy

LEADERSHIP AND THE SIN OF EMPATHY

COMPASSION AND ITS COUNTERFEITS

JOE RIGNEY

MOSCOW, IDAHO

Published by Canon Press
P.O. Box 8729, Moscow, Idaho 83843
800.488.2034 | www.canonpress.com

Cover design by James Engerbretson
Interior design by Belle Iverson

Chapters 1, 2, 3, and 6 appeared in a previous form on desiringgod.org.
Sections of Chapter 4 appeared in a previous form on wng.org and desiringgod.org.
Chapter 5 appeared in a previous form on americanreformer.org.
Sections of Appendix A appeared in a previous form on desiringgod.org.
Appendix B appeared in a previous form on desiringgod.org.

Printed in Canada.

Library of Congress Cataloging-in-Publication Data for the first edition is on file with the publisher.

25 26 27 28 29 30 31 32 33 34 10 9 8 7 6 5 4 3 2 1

To the Doddses and Nasellis

CONTENTS

Foreword *ix*

Introduction *xiii*

1 What Does Empathy Mean? *1*

2 Weaponizing Pity *17*

3 The Sins of Empaths *31*

4 Life Under the Progressive Gaze *47*

5 Feminism: Queen of the Woke *77*

6 In Praise of Compassion *101*

Appendix A. On Provocative Rhetoric: "The Sin of Empathy" 119

Appendix B. Corrupt Compassion: Recognizing a Devilish Strategy 127

About the Author 141

FOREWORD

WHAT DOES CHRISTIAN LOVE LOOK LIKE when you see someone drowning in a river?

Should he who stands safely on shore turn away in hard-hearted callousness, leaving the victim to suffer alone and without rescue?

Should he "hold space" for the victim, suspending judgment, relinquishing the search for solutions, and instead jumping in the river and joining in this watery death?

Should he secure himself to the land and toss a rope, even climbing down the bank tethered to the secured rope, courageously drawing the victim safely to shore?

In the first example, the hard-hearted observer feels no moral responsibility to the man in crisis. "Not my problem," he says as he walks away.

In the second example, the empathetic observer seeks to affirm the victim's feelings and joins the victim in the problem. "Suffering together" takes priority over problem-solving.

In the third example, the sympathetic observer identifies and solves the problem by tethering himself to something more lasting and substantial than the victim's feelings. He cares for the potential victim in body, soul, and emotions and carefully executes a rescue plan.

Leadership and The Sin of Empathy: Compassion and Its Counterfeits makes a case for virtuous, compassionate Christian sympathy, which binds itself to biblical truth and courageously brings others out of darkness into light. Joe Rigney is not against empathy—the ability to appreciate and respect the feelings of another—but he does take issue with untethered empathy—an emotive connection that exceeds and overpowers reality and good judgment. In this short book, he defines his terms carefully and swims against the tide by rejecting the popular notion that untethered empathy is compassion's prerequisite.

When the broad evangelical church embraces untethered empathy, it renders Christians incapable of thinking through basic categories: Does pro-life mean protecting infants in the womb or illegals at the Southern border? Do government schools bless Christians or challenge their First Amendment rights? Is homosexuality a sin, found in the flesh, forbidden in the law of God, and overcome by the Savior, or is it a personhood group with an immutable but morally neutral untapped blessing to be stewarded and sanctified, rendering queer treasures in heaven? When empathy is unhitched from the Truth, it becomes an idol and a god. And feelings create tyrannical idols and gods.

Because a Christian needs to distinguish the counterfeit from the real, Pastor Rigney begins by identifying how virtues go wrong—how untethered empathy defaults into manipulation. Before the reader balks at this, consider that the famed "love chapter" in the Bible (1 Corinthians 13) begins with pervasive negativity: "Love does *not* envy, love does *not* parade itself, is *not* puffed up; does *not* behave rudely, does *not* seek its own, is *not* provoked, thinks *no* evil, does *not* rejoice in iniquity" (vs. 4–6). Knowing what love is *not* is necessary to understand what love is. Untethered empathy shipwrecks Christian lives. Indeed, it creates moral failure wherever it resides. Untethered empathy is not Christian love.

Those who know the author know that Joe wears many hats: professor, academician, college administrator, C.S. Lewis scholar, aficionado of all Great Books, and master of biblical theology and the well-turned phrase. But this book is authored by *Pastor* Joe Rigney. His concern on every page is your soul and God's glory. Pastor Joe Rigney serves as an able trail guide through the challenging disciplines of cognitive neuroscience, systematic theology, biblical theology, and cultural apologetics, culminating in a rich and helpful analysis of how the virtue of empathy can devolve into treachery despite good intentions. This book is not some heady treatise for the erudite elite but soul food for those wondering how we got to a place where feelings reign triumphantly, and everything else serves as a handmaid.

Pastor Joe Rigney does more than identify problems. He offers real solutions, the kind that anyone who dearly loves a prodigal needs. Every page reveals Jesus as our model of genuine Christian compassion: "I am the resurrection and the life. Whoever believes in me, though he die, yet shall he live, and everyone who lives and believes in me shall never die" (John 11:25–26). Joe echoes these precious words of Jesus in the final words of this beautiful book, reminding us that God's people rest in God's love, where truth anchors our compassion (John 8:31–32).

Rosaria Butterfield
Christmas 2024

INTRODUCTION

A CHILD SULKS IN HIS ROOM AFTER hitting his sister, hoping to avoid punishment from his parents.

A woman puts her family on a guilt trip for their unwillingness to come home for Thanksgiving.

A man attempts to cover up sexual abuse by telling his victim, "Don't tell anyone; I'll get in so much trouble."

A group of "nice" elders urges the senior pastor to avoid certain topics in his preaching, lest he offend certain members of a Racial Reconciliation Task Force.

A doctor pressures a mother and father to affirm their child's newfound gender identity, asking, "Would you rather have a dead son, or a live daughter?"

Each of these situations has a common thread: the attempted manipulation of someone else's pity. Pity, of course, is a good thing. It spurs us to help those who are hurting. But unmoored from what is good and right, pity becomes destructive. Compassion degenerates into untethered empathy, leaving destruction in its wake. And given the prevalence of appeals to empathy in our society, it's vital that we learn to distinguish good from bad, healthy from toxic, the virtue of compassion from the sin of empathy.

This book might be thought of as a prequel to its companion, *Leadership and Emotional Sabotage*, an elaboration on one of the steering wheels that people use to derail leaders and their institutions. Both books have a backstory. Both began with Edwin Friedman and his seminal work *A Failure of Nerve: Leadership in the Age of the Quick Fix*.[1] I purchased it in August 2011 for use in a college class on Christian leadership which I was teaching. I found the book to be provocative, insightful, and full of practical wisdom.

It was Friedman who first alerted me to the dangers of empathy and its triumph in the modern world. Friedman argued that empathy today is often "a disguise for

1. Edwin H. Friedman, *A Failure of Nerve: Leadership in the Age of the Quick Fix* (New York: Seabury, 2007); and Joe Rigney, *Leadership and Emotional Sabotage: Resisting the Anxiety That Will Wreck Your Family, Destroy Your Church, and Ruin the World* (Moscow, ID: Canon Press, 2024).

anxiety . . . and a power tool in the hands of the sensitive."[2] Though the term "empathy" is of recent vintage, Friedman argued that, in recent years, empathy has become a sacred cow, one which allows the least mature and most reactive members of a community to hijack the community's agenda.[3]

Needless to say, I found Friedman compelling and proceeded to teach from his book (though not uncritically) for the next five years or so. Part of Friedman's strength is his use of concrete and relatable situations to support his claims. My students and I wrestled with Friedman's illustrations, asking how Christians ought to faithfully respond to such situations, and how to translate Friedman's insights into Christian categories and language.

Meanwhile, the world seemed to be conspiring to prove Friedman's thesis. Everywhere I looked, I saw evidence of chronic anxiety, a herd mentality, and low thresholds for emotional pain and distress. Passions were in the driver's seat, and there was an unfortunate lack of sober-minded, self-differentiated leadership in both the wider culture and the church.

In the summer of 2018, I was invited to speak at a student conference in Moscow, Idaho. As an addendum, the organizers asked if I would be willing to be the first guest on a new talk show they were piloting called *Man Rampant* (in the mold of William F. Buckley's *Firing Line*), with Doug Wilson as the host. Since Doug and I shared

2. Friedman, *A Failure of Nerve*, 133.

3. Friedman, *A Failure of Nerve*, 136.

an appreciation for Friedman, I suggested the topic "The Sin of Empathy."[4] We filmed the episode in July 2018, and it was released in October 2019. It provoked a wide range of reactions. Some people appreciated the distinctions and categories we offered. Others were honestly confused by the definitions and terms in play; they struggled to even grasp the possibility that empathy could be dangerous or sinful. At the same time, the visceral reaction of others seemed to validate the argument. It was as though people had decided to light their hair on fire in response to a warning about flammable heads. Still others seized the opportunity afforded by the confusion to willfully misrepresent what we had discussed.

Since that time, I've written multiple articles, preached sermons and conference messages, and participated in dozens of interviews and conversations in which I've sought to build out and clarify what I mean by the sin of empathy. This book is the fruit of that labor. It's a distillation of the tens of thousands of words that I've written on empathy and compassion over the last several years.

Perhaps the simplest way to introduce the subject is through two sets of biblical passages. On the one hand, the Scriptures command us to have sympathy and a tender heart (1 Pet. 3:8). Paul tells us to clothe ourselves in compassion (Col. 3:12; literally, "bowels of mercy"). He tells the Philippians that he yearns for them "with the affection

4. Doug Wilson and Joe Rigney, *Man Rampant*, Season 1, Episode 1, "The Sin of Empathy," Canon Press, March 18, 2021, YouTube video, 1:07:45, https://www.youtube.com/watch?v=6i9a3Rfd7yI.

of Christ" (Phil. 1:8). The Greek word for "affection" here, *splankna*, connotes a depth of feeling, loving someone from the gut. According to Paul, such affection and sympathy are bonding agents, enabling us to be single-minded and in one accord (Phil. 2:1).

What's more, God has given us families so that we learn the meaning of these terms by personal experience:

> Can a woman forget her nursing child,
>   that she should have no compassion on the son of her womb?
> Even these may forget,
>   yet I will not forget you. (Isa. 49:15)

> As a father shows compassion to his children, so the LORD shows compassion to those who fear him. (Ps. 103:13)

In both of these passages, the assumption is that fathers and mothers have deep feeling and compassion for their children. More than that, the compassion of parents points to the compassion of God. Compassion is so central to who God is that he reveals it as his name: "The LORD—the LORD is a compassionate and gracious God, slow to anger and abounding in faithful love and truth" (Ex. 34:6, CSB). Compassion, sympathy, pity—these are attributes of God, attributes that he has communicated to us through our families in order that we might be characterized by deep affection and bowels of mercy.

On the other hand, the Bible contains passages like this:

> If your brother, the son of your mother, or your son or your daughter or the wife you embrace or your friend who is as your own soul entices you secretly, saying, "Let us go and serve other gods," which neither you nor your fathers have known, some of the gods of the peoples who are around you, whether near you or far off from you, from the one end of the earth to the other, you shall not yield to him or listen to him, nor shall your eye pity him, nor shall you spare him, nor shall you conceal him. But you shall kill him. Your hand shall be first against him to put him to death, and afterward the hand of all the people. (Deut. 13:6–9)

In this passage, we are forbidden to show pity or compassion on those who would entice us to idolatry. Similar commands are given with respect to first-degree murder and lying in court (Deut. 7:16; 19:13; 19:21). In such cases, God is adamant that "your eye shall not pity them." Notice how God piles up the familial terms. He's telling us, "I know what I'm asking—sometimes you must overcome natural emotions in order to be faithful to me." And here as well, we are following God as our model, who executes his judgment *without* pity or compassion:

> Therefore, as I live, declares the Lord GOD, surely, because you have defiled my sanctuary with all your detestable things and with all your abominations, therefore I will withdraw. My eye will not spare, and I will have no pity. (Ezek. 5:11)

> And my eye will not spare you, nor will I have pity, but I will punish you for your ways, while your abominations are in your midst. Then you will know that I am the LORD. (Ezek. 7:4; see also Ezek. 7:9; 8:18; Jer. 13:14; Lam. 2:17)

So then, we are to be characterized by tenderhearted compassion and pity (like God), and yet there are times when pity and compassion are strictly and absolutely forbidden. It's this second principle that is difficult for many moderns to accept. The idea that pity and compassion could ever be sinful, could ever be inappropriate and wrong, is almost blasphemous in the modern world. And as a result, the modern world has sought to give compassion an upgrade, to improve it and make it more loving. Enter empathy ("All rise"). This book is about that shift—the shift from compassion to empathy—and how it wreaks havoc on families, churches, relationships, and societies.

The structure of the book is as follows. In chapter 1, I begin with definitions, highlighting the various ways that the term "empathy" has been defined and clarifying the way that I will be using it in this book. In chapter 2, I describe how empathy turns love into hatred, using examples from *The Great Divorce*. In chapter 3, I show how untethered empathy leads to cowardice, indifference, and cruelty.

In chapter 4, I describe the specific ways that sly pagans and professing Christians have used empathy, credibility, and respectability to sabotage the church over the last fifteen years or so, particularly in relation to issues of race, gender, and abuse. Chapter 5 continues this exploration, noting the way that feminism feeds these destructive dynamics, both in the church and in society. Finally, lest there be any mistake, in chapter 6, I praise the virtue of compassion, offering counsel on how to comfort the hurting like Christ does.

I've also included two appendices. Appendix A answers one of the more common objections to my writings on empathy: namely, the use of provocative rhetoric. Some critics, including friends of mine, have agreed with my substantive points about the dangers of empathy but regard the phrase "the sin of empathy" as unhelpful, confusing, and needlessly provocative. So if you've stumbled over the title of this book, you might start there.

Appendix B includes my first foray into this subject, two articles written in the style of Lewis's *Screwtape Letters*, originally published at Desiring God. I include them for two reasons. First, I thoroughly enjoyed writing them, and I like to share things that I enjoy. Second, together they capture the heart of this book. Almost everything in here is present in seed form in those first two articles, and thus it seemed worthwhile to include them.

Finally, it's worth noting that I write this book, not as a scholar, but as a pastor. I'm concerned first and foremost, not with the "true" definition of empathy, but with its use. It's the emotional and relational dynamics that I'm attempting to address, whatever you call them. I believe that there are perfectly good applications of the term "empathy," such as when psychologists use the term in treating autism, or when it is popularly used as a rough synonym for compassion and sympathy. My fundamental issue is with empathy as it is practiced and weaponized in the church and in the culture. I've seen the destructiveness firsthand, and I would like to commend the biblical virtue of compassion in the face of its counterfeit, for the good of others and the glory of God.

1
WHAT DOES EMPATHY MEAN?

IF YOU LOOK UP HEBREWS 4:15 IN A number of different English translations, you will find that most of them use the word "sympathize" to describe Christ's posture toward our weaknesses. For example, the ESV reads, "We do not have a high priest who is unable to *sympathize* with our weaknesses, but one who in every respect has been tempted as we are, yet without sin." The Greek word in question is *sympathizo*, which makes the English cognate a natural choice. The NASB, NKJV, CSB, and NET all follow suit in their translations. When we look up Hebrews 4:15 in the NIV, however, we read this:

> We do not have a high priest who is unable to *empathize* with our weaknesses, but we have one who has been tempted in every way, just as we are—yet he did not sin.

The NIV's translation decision reflects a broader cultural shift away from sympathy and toward empathy. At one level, this is a very small change, the substitution of one prefix for another. "Sympathy" (and its Latin equivalent, "compassion") literally means "suffering with" (*sym* + *pathos* in Greek, *com* + *passio* in Latin; throughout this book, I will use sympathy and compassion interchangeably). "Empathy," on the other hand, means "suffering in."

The argument of this book is that the shift from "with" to "in" is of more than philological importance. At stake is the difference between virtue and vice, goodness and sin. While many struggle to fathom how empathy could go wrong, I intend to argue that all sorts of toxic, pathological, and sinful behaviors can hide beneath seemingly innocuous terms. So let's begin with the challenge of definition.

Defining Empathy

The term "empathy" itself is very recent. It was introduced into English in the early twentieth century in the field of aesthetics. It originally meant "feeling in," and it referred to the ability to project one's own imagined feelings into the world (a definition that is almost the opposite of its contemporary meaning). In 1955, *Reader's Digest* defined the term as "the ability to appreciate the other person's feelings without yourself becoming so emotionally involved that your judgment is affected."[1]

A 2020 article by a leading psychology professor in *Scientific American* describes the difficulty in defining empathy like this:

> Empathy is a fundamentally squishy term. Like many broad and complicated concepts, empathy can mean many things. Even the researchers who study it do not always say what they mean, or measure empathy in the same way in their studies—and they definitely do not agree on a definition. In fact, there are stark contradictions: what one researcher calls empathy is not empathy to another.[2]

This difficulty doesn't merely plague researchers and specialists. It also afflicts laymen:

> When laypeople are surveyed on how they define empathy, the range of answers is wide as well. Some people think empathy is a feeling; others focus on what a person does or says. Some think it is being good at reading someone's

1. Susan Lanzoni, "A Short History of Empathy," *The Atlantic*, October 15, 2015, https://www.theatlantic.com/health/archive/2015/10/a-short-history-of-empathy/409912/.

2. Judith A. Hall and Mark Leary, "The U.S. Has an Empathy Deficit," *Scientific American*, September 17, 2020, https://www.scientificamerican.com/article/the-us-has-an-empathy-deficit/.

> nonverbal cues, while others include the mental orientation of putting oneself in someone else's shoes. Still others see empathy as the ability or effort to imagine others' feelings, or as just feeling "connected" or "relating" to someone. Some think it is a moral stance to be concerned about other people's welfare and a desire to help them out. Sometimes it seems like "empathy" is just another way of saying "being a nice and decent person." Actions, feelings, perspectives, motives, values—all of these are "empathy" according to someone.[3]

A recent article in the *Journal of Social Psychology* notes the difficulty of evaluating the success of empathy as a concept in social and personal psychology.[4] Put simply, the term has no agreed-upon definition. In the article, the authors note a number of possible definitions:

- knowing another's thoughts and feelings;
- imagining another's thoughts and feelings;
- adopting the posture of another;
- actually feeling as another does;
- imagining how one would feel or think in another's place;
- feeling distress at another's suffering;
- feeling for another's suffering, sometimes called pity or compassion;
- projecting oneself into another's situation.

3. Hall and Leary, "Empathy Deficit."
4. Judith A. Hall and Rachel Schwartz, "Empathy Present and Future," *Journal of Social Psychology* 159, no. 3 (2018): 225–243, doi:10.1080/00224545.2018.1477442.

Generally speaking, these different definitions fall into one of three categories. First, empathy is sometimes defined as an intentional *cognitive* act. It's the ability to see things from other people's point of view, to really understand what and how they think. An empathetic person is able to "put themselves in another's shoes." This cognitive understanding of empathy is sometimes called "perspective-taking."

Second, empathy sometimes refers to an affective or emotional act. It's not merely knowing what someone feels, but actually feeling what they feel. If they are happy, I'm happy. If they are sad, I'm sad. The affectional definition of empathy is called "emotion-sharing."

Finally, empathy may refer not to sharing the same emotion as another person but instead to the warm feelings we have for those in distress (under this definition, empathy is sometimes equated with compassion or sympathy). In both of the affective or emotional definitions, this "feeling in" may be voluntary; we choose to immerse ourselves in the emotions of another person. At other times, it is involuntary; empathetic people are highly sensitive to the emotions of others and can be overcome by them, whether they want to be or not.

In sum, part of the trouble with empathy is that there is so little agreement about its proper definition.

Brené Brown and the Sin of Sympathy

But as I noted in the introduction, this book is not primarily interested in the "true" definition of empathy, but rather with its use and influence in our culture. To explore that, we must look at a highly influential video by author Brené Brown.

The three-minute YouTube video has been viewed over 22 million times.[5] It has been used in ministry training seminars and college classrooms. Taken from a larger talk called "The Power of Vulnerability," Brown sets out to commend empathy as essential for human connection. While some people argue that empathy is simply a synonym for sympathy, Brown insists that empathy and sympathy are very different. In fact, her video might well have been titled "The Sin of Sympathy."

Brown argues that sympathy drives disconnection. Sympathy stands aloof from suffering. It attempts to find silver linings in the afflictions of others, but refuses to join them in their sadness. Empathy, on the other hand, fuels connection. Empathy includes perspective-taking, by which Brown means recognizing someone's perspective as "their truth." It "stays out of judgment," recognizing emotion in other people, and then communicating that recognition. Empathy is a "sacred space" in which we join people in their darkness and refuse to find silver linings in their affliction. (Interestingly, Brown defines empathy as "feeling *with* people," not "feeling *in* people.")

For Brown, sympathy highlights an asymmetry in the relationship—there is a sufferer and a comforter, someone in the pit and someone attempting to help them out.

5. "Brené Brown on Empathy," Royal Society for the Encouragement of Arts, Manufactures, and Commerce, December 10, 2013, YouTube video, 2:53, https://www.youtube.com/watch?v=1Evwgu369Jw.

Empathy, on the other hand, minimizes that sense of asymmetry both by withholding judgment and by resisting the urge to make things better by responding to the despairing words of sufferers. Instead, we simply sit in the dark with them and listen, making the vulnerable choice to share their emotions.

Evaluating Brown

Now there are clearly praiseworthy aspects of Brown's video. It's good to try to understand others, to see things from their point of view, to recognize their "felt reality." It's good to feel the same emotions as other people—to weep with those who weep and rejoice with those who rejoice (Rom. 12:15). It's good to feel warm and compassionate emotions for those in distress (and hopefully be moved to help them in concrete ways).

However, Brown commends these good acts at the expense of sympathy, and we ought to pause before we relegate the virtue of sympathy or pity to the trash heap. So let's consider what is occurring in the elevation of empathy over sympathy.

As I noted above, "sympathy" is an English word borrowed directly from the Greek word *sympathizo*. Like its Latin cognate, "compassion," it means "to suffer with" or "to feel with" (Greek = *sym* + *pathos*; Latin = *com* + *passio*). So as a first clue to the significance of the shift, let's ask, "What's the difference between saying that we should suffer *with* others and saying that we should suffer *in* them?"

Both words concern our orientation to hurting and suffering people, but they represent this orientation differently. Sympathy willingly joins with sufferers in their pain. Empathy makes their suffering our own in a more universal and totalizing way. This, in fact, is why some commend empathy as a more loving response to the pain of others. To suffer or feel *with* someone maintains a certain kind of emotional separation or boundary between the comforter and the afflicted; we're with them, but we're not *in them*. We maintain our own personal integrity and boundaries—I remain I, and you remain you.

For authors like Brown, the emotional distance of sympathy is the problem that empathy overcomes. Empathy encourages a greater fusion of my emotions and the emotions of the afflicted. For many, empathy's virtue (and its superiority over sympathy) lies precisely in this fuller immersion in the pain and feelings of another, in so entering into their experience that we fully feel what they feel. As Brown's video suggested, sympathy preserves a kind of asymmetry between comforter and afflicted, whereas empathy attempts to minimize this asymmetry by withholding judgment and evaluation.

The Sin of Apathy

Now at this point, it's important to note that the emotional boundaries implied in sympathy could become a problem. Instead of sympathy, we could have apathy, a callous refusal to identify with and share the pain and suffering of others. No weeping with those who weep. No "compassionate hearts" or "bowels of mercy" (Col. 3:12). Instead of opening our hearts to those in distress, we might close them, and thus demonstrate that the love of God is not in us (1 John 3:17–18). The apathetic are numb to the pain of others, standing aloof, detached, and unmoved by their suffering.

Hard-hearted and self-centered apathy is one danger. Anxious apathy is another. At times, our refusal to sympathize with the hurting is rooted in the fear of strong emotion. When faced with deep distress in others, we frequently don't know what to do. We find their sadness or grief or anxiety intolerable, and we either try to steer them out of it against their will or withdraw from them and shut down. Our anxious attempts to find silver linings are driven by our own agitation. Think of the way that biblical truth (such as "God works all things together for good") is sometimes wielded as correction instead of comfort. Rather than sharing the sufferer's sorrow, we try to alter their theology in the moment of their pain. We offer pontificating correction disguised as ham-fisted comfort because we find their pain overwhelming. In that respect, Brown's warnings about sympathy are well-taken. Often the best immediate response to deep suffering is a simple and heartfelt acknowledgement that the pain is real and deep. Or perhaps no words at all, just presence and tears.

Reacting or Responding?

But the emotional boundaries and separation implied in sympathy and compassion can serve another purpose. They allow the comforter to maintain the kind of stability and sober-mindedness necessary to actually help the sufferer. Alastair Roberts has distinguished empathy from compassion in this way: empathy is often fundamentally or primarily oriented to the *feelings* of sufferers; compassion (or sympathy) is fundamentally or primarily oriented to their *good*.[6]

Because empathy is an emotive connection closely tied to the immediate feelings of the hurting, it is fundamentally reactive. It leaps to alleviate what seems to be the most visible cause of suffering (and thus sometimes mistakes a symptom for the root). Sympathy, on the other hand, is fundamentally responsive. It maintains enough emotional space to consider the picture as a whole and not get lost in the immediate acuteness of the suffering. As a result, it is able to take sober-minded and carefully considered action to address others' pain. In this sense, the "separation" involved in sympathy and compassion is rooted not in apathy, but in a deep desire for the good of the afflicted. What's more, sympathy is humble since it recognizes that the hot emotion of the present moment may not be the whole story. In fact, that hot emotion may blur our vision of what is most needful.

6. Alastair Roberts, "An Ethic of Nerve and Compassion," *Alistair's Adversaria,* May 27, 2013, https://alastairadversaria.com/2013/05/27/an-ethic-of-nerve-and-compassion/.

Since empathy entails a suspension of judgment and a more comprehensive sharing of emotion, then the danger of empathy is drowning in the pain and suffering of another. If a sufferer is sinking in quicksand, an empathetic helper jumps in after them with both feet. A sympathetic helper, on the other hand, steps into the quicksand with one foot while keeping the other firmly planted on the shore (there's the emotional boundary). Sympathy lays hold of something sturdy outside of the pit in order to provide an anchor, so that we can better help the one in the quicksand.[7]

This danger is particularly acute for those who are naturally empathetic—those who are highly sensitive to the emotions of others and therefore easily swallowed by their grief and distress. What's more, sufferers frequently make unreasonable demands of those who are trying to help them. After we've climbed down into the pit with them, they demand that we agree there is no way out. They may even demand that we destroy the ladder we are offering them. And empathy, in its zeal to stay out of

7. In her book *Dare to Lead*, Brené Brown, in commending empathy, identifies precisely this danger: "If to struggle is to be down in a hole, empathy is not jumping into the hole with someone who is struggling and taking on their emotions or owning their struggle as yours to fix. If their issues become yours, now you have two people stuck in a hole. Not helpful. Boundaries are important here. We have to know where we end and others begin if we really want to show up with empathy." Brené Brown, *Dare to Lead: Brave Work. Tough Conversations. Whole Hearts.* (New York: Random House, 2018), 142. While the warning against jumping in with both feet is well-taken, it seems to jar with what Brown says elsewhere about "staying out of judgment" and climbing into the pit with those who are hurting.

judgment, is often willing to burn the ladder in the name of fueling connection.

On Virtues and How They Go Wrong

What then can we conclude from this initial survey? To begin, as Christians, we ought to resist any move to disparage biblical virtues. Sympathy, pity, compassion—these are biblical words with a long and well-developed history in the Christian tradition. The contemporary push to elevate empathy is frequently tied to the demotion and denigration of these other terms. Empathy, we're told, is Sympathy 2.0, Upgraded Compassion, and we are free to dispense with the beta version. This chapter has pointed out some of the problems with this so-called upgrade. The rest of the book will show how these problems are wrecking Western civilization, from families to churches to whole societies.

As a result, in this book, I will use the term "empathy" in one of two ways. The first is simply as "emotion-sharing." Emotion-sharing in itself is neither virtuous nor vicious. It's simply a common feature of human relationships. In this sense, it is a natural emotion, and not necessarily a virtue.

The second and more negative use is the sin of (untethered) empathy, which is the excessive and overpowering form of this passion. To clarify this use, consider how virtues work.

Virtue often involves the faithful stewardship of our passions. Passions are the impulsive and powerful snap reactions that we have to reality. They are good, but dangerous. God designed us so that our minds would rule and govern our passions. God over mind; mind over passions. Virtue requires us to faithfully and habitually cultivate, steward, govern, guide, and master our passions in obedience to God.

Consider a virtue like courage. Courage is the habitual self-possession that subdues fear by the power of a deeper desire for a greater good.[8] Courage involves a sort of double vision. On the one hand, there is the objective danger that produces a subjective passion: fear. On the other hand, there is an objective good that produces a deep desire. Courage is when we pursue that greater good in the face of the danger and fear. Ultimately, Christian courage insists that the greater good is God himself: "Be strong and courageous . . . for the LORD your God is with you wherever you go" (Josh. 1:9). Christ is the greater good, the joy set before us, that enables us to overcome fear and anxiety. By clinging to him, we subdue our fears.

Virtues go wrong through either deficiency or excess. A deficiency of courage is cowardice. Cowardice shrinks back from danger. It succumbs to the passion of fear and therefore refuses to take risks, or it retreats in the face of pain, difficulty, and death. On the other hand, recklessness or rashness is an excess of courage. It refuses to be governed by wisdom and therefore takes foolish and unnecessary risks. Courage maintains the proper balance. It's guided by

8. For a book-length treatment of courage, see Joe Rigney, *Courage: How the Gospel Creates Christian Fortitude* (Wheaton, IL: Crossway, 2023).

reason and wisdom; it recognizes what should and should not be feared, and it keeps the bigger picture in view. Courage distinguishes between necessary and unnecessary risks.

Turning to the subject of this book, the virtue of compassion (or sympathy) is the habitual inclination to share the suffering and pain of the hurting that moves us to relieve their suffering and pursue their ultimate good. Like courage, it has a double vision. It sees the objective affliction and the subjective misery of a sufferer, and it resolves to join them in their pain. At the same time, it remains anchored to what is good and thus desires to relieve their suffering by pursuing their true well-being. The biblical imperative is to weep with those who weep, to clothe ourselves with "bowels of mercy," to relieve suffering because, like Christ, we are "moved with compassion."

So also compassion goes wrong through deficiency or excess. A deficiency of compassion is apathy, that callous refusal to identify with and share the pain and suffering of others. On the other hand, empathy is an excess of compassion, when our identification with and sharing of the emotions of others overwhelms our minds and sweeps us off our feet. Empathy loses sight of the ultimate good, both for ourselves and for the hurting.

To use another analogy, if a person is drowning in a river with a strong current, apathy is unmoved and therefore refuses to help at all. Empathy is overwhelmed by the danger and dives in and is swept away by the current. True compassion tethers itself to the shore with a rope and swims to the drowning man with a life preserver.

Both errors are related to the notion of tethering. Apathy stands on the shore, but refuses to connect with the sufferer. Empathy dives in to connect with the sufferer, but loses touch with the shore. The virtue of compassion or sympathy insists on being tethered to both.

And this untethering is precisely our challenge. As Chesterton put it:

> The modern world is full of the old Christian virtues gone mad. The virtues have gone mad because they have been isolated from each other and are wandering alone. Thus some scientists care for truth; and their truth is pitiless. Thus some humanitarians only care for pity; and their pity (I am sorry to say) is often untruthful.[9]

Untruthful pity. Untethered empathy. These are the counterfeits of compassion.

9. G.K. Chesterton, *Orthodoxy*, (Moscow: Canon Press, 2020), 28.

2
WEAPONIZING PITY

C.S. LEWIS BEGINS HIS BOOK *THE FOUR Loves* with the observation of De Rougemont that "love ceases to be a demon only when he ceases to be a god." Or, in Lewis's restatement, "love begins to be a demon the moment he begins to be a god."[1]

Lewis is concerned that human love tends to claim for itself a divine authority that overrides all other obligations. It demands unconditional allegiance and

1. C.S. Lewis, *The Four Loves* (New York: HarperOne, 2017).

thereby becomes a demon that destroys both us and itself.

Significantly for Lewis, a natural love only makes this claim when it is at its highest, at those moments when it most resembles God. Its claim to divinity is only plausible if there is a real likeness between it and Love himself. But having become a deity, it becomes a demon, and as a demon, it ceases to be love at all but instead becomes a very complicated form of hatred.

The Great Divorce

To illustrate the point, we might consider a recurring character in Lewis's writings: the tyrannical and possessive mother. In *The Four Loves*, she is called Mrs. Fidget. In *The Screwtape Letters*, she is described as "the sort of woman who lives for others—you can always tell the others by their hunted expression."[2] And in *The Great Divorce*, she is called Pam, a ghost who lost her son Michael as a boy.

It is this last example that I wish to use as an illustration. *The Great Divorce* is Lewis's version of Dante's *Divine Comedy*, where the narrator has a dream about the afterlife in which he converses with the souls of the damned and the redeemed. In the dream, it's possible for the damned ghosts to repent and turn to Christ and thereby become Solid Spirits. We witness one ghost do so, allowing an angel to kill the lust that is enslaving him. The purpose of the book is to clarify the nature of the Choice faced by every

2. C.S. Lewis, *The Screwtape Letters* (New York: Harper Collins, 2009), 145.

human being: will we put God at the center of our lives, or will we put ourselves there?[3] In Lewis's words, "If we insist on keeping hell (or even earth) we shall not see heaven: if we accept heaven we shall not be able to retain even the smallest and most intimate souvenirs of hell."[4]

Returning to Pam, we are told that her love for her lost son Michael is "uncontrolled and fierce and monomaniac."[5] When she meets her brother Reginald on the green plains, she is put out because Michael has not come to meet her. Reginald, who is there to lead her to the Mountains (Heaven), insists that she must be "thickened up a bit" before Michael will be able to see her. The thickening process begins with her desiring Someone Else besides Michael.

Pam sullenly agrees to try "religion and all that sort of thing," but only so that they will hurry up and let her see her boy. In other words, she attempts to use God as a means to Michael. Her love is intensely possessive: "I want my boy, and I mean to have him. He is mine, do you understand? Mine, mine, mine, for ever and ever."[6] This is a twisted form of the rightful affection that a mother has for her son. A child does belong to his mother, in some

3. For a more detailed account of *The Great Divorce* and the theme of the Choice in Lewis's writings, see Joe Rigney, *Lewis on the Christian Life: Becoming Truly Human in the Presence of God* (Crossway, 2018).

4. C.S. Lewis, *The Great Divorce* (1946; repr., New York: HarperOne, 2015), viii–ix.

5. Lewis, *The Great Divorce*, 100.

6. Lewis, *The Great Divorce*, 103.

sense. But when natural affection becomes a god, it makes a total and ultimate claim to ownership.

What's more, Pam's love for Michael has the appearance of sacrifice but is, in fact, a complicated form of hatred. She protests that she gave up her whole life for Michael, that she sacrificed everything for his memory. But George MacDonald, Lewis's guide in *The Great Divorce*, points out that her love is not excessive but defective. She would rather have her son with her in Hell than give up possession of him. She would rather possess her son in everlasting misery than release him into everlasting joy. Hatred is not too strong a word.

Lewis takes pains to remind us that the corruption of such loves is greater because their natural goodness is greater. Mother-love is a grand and glorious virtue. Therefore, when it goes bad—when it becomes a god—it becomes a terrifying demon indeed.

Passion of Pity

Lewis applied this principle to the three natural loves: *storge* (familial affection), *eros* (romantic or sexual love), and *philia* (love between friends). But in principle, he notes that the same can be applied to many other kinds of love—love of country and love of nature, for example. Pam's story points to another surprising form of corrupted love, what Lewis calls "the passion of pity."[7]

7. Lewis, *The Great Divorce*, 118.

The passion of pity is what happens when love for the hurting, the broken, and the weak (what we typically call compassion) becomes a god, and in doing so, becomes a demon.

We see subtle indications of the complicated dynamics when compassion goes wrong in Pam's conversation with Reginald. Recall that Pam was attempting to use God as a means to see her son Michael. When Reginald confronts Pam about her selfishness, Pam rebuffs him with her own suffering as a mother. And when Reginald reminds her of God's love and suffering on her behalf, Pam responds, "If he loved me, he'd let me see my boy."[8] Pam is appealing to a certain definition of love, a love that does whatever the beloved wants, especially if she has suffered.

Now, it's important to get straight on this situation. Pam really has objectively suffered. Her beloved son Michael was ripped from her through death. She continued to feel the pain of his loss long after his death, even as she learned to "expect no sympathy" from her husband and daughter, who, in her mind, didn't truly care for Michael or for her.[9] That's her lived and experienced reality as a bereaved mother.

But this doesn't change the truth that her high and holy mother-love was actually tyrannical. Living only for Michael's memory was a mistake (and, according to Reginald, she knows it). Her husband and daughter

8. Lewis, *The Great Divorce*, 91.

9. Lewis, *The Great Divorce*, 95.

genuinely loved Michael—they only rebelled against Pam's attempts to dominate them with her pain. Her insistence on clinging to the past was, in fact, "the wrong way to deal with a sorrow."[10]

The Wrong Way to Deal with Pain

Pam's response to Reginald's correction is telling: "You are heartless. Everyone is heartless." And then, sarcastically, she says, "Oh, of course. I'm wrong. Everything I say or do is wrong, according to you." Pam is attempting to use her suffering (both real and imagined) as a way to get what she wants from Reginald. In her grief, she sulks and pouts in order to elicit compassion from her brother. But then, as Pam erupts at Reginald and at God, we see this key interaction.

> "I hate your religion, and I hate and despise your God. I believe in a God of love."
>
> "And yet, Pam, you have no love at this moment for your own mother or for me."
>
> "Oh, I see! That's the trouble, is it? Really, Reginald! The idea of your being hurt because. . ."
>
> "Lord love you!" said the Spirit with a great laugh. "You needn't bother about that! Don't you know that you can't hurt anyone in this country?"
>
> The Ghost was silent and open-mouthed for a moment; more wilted, I thought, by this re-assurance than by anything else that had been said.[11]

10. Lewis, *The Great Divorce*, 95.
11. Lewis, *The Great Divorce*, 103–104.

In this moment, Pam realizes that she can no longer use her suffering to hurt and manipulate those who love her. A weapon has been taken out of her hand. Unable to hurt Reginald or weaponize his pity, she is at a loss for words.

Love Measured by Misery

Pam is not the only character in *The Great Divorce* who seeks to steer others through their compassion. Lewis's most extended display of this emotional tactic occurs at the end of the book in the conversation between the ghost Frank and the saint Sarah Smith, who was his wife on earth.

When they first meet, Frank acts as though he's concerned about the misery of his wife in his absence. He wears his compassion on his sleeve. "It's not myself I'm thinking about. It is you. That is what has been continually on my mind—all these years. The thought of you—you here alone, breaking your heart about me."[12] However, as he discovers that she has not been miserable in his absence, he grows offended. He contemplates overlooking the "offense," but wonders whether she'll notice his sacrifice. (After all, there was that time on earth when he let her use the last postage stamp, even though he needed to mail a letter himself—and she didn't notice.) So he persists in attempting to comfort her in her misery, and then (like Pam) is frustrated to discover that there are no miseries in Heaven. It becomes clear

12. Lewis, *The Great Divorce*, 122.

through the remainder of the conversation that he views Sarah's misery as a measure of her love for him. He is only interested in a love that desperately needs him and that he can manipulate to get his way.

Emotional Blackmail

Frank resists all attempts by Sarah to draw him out of his selfishness. Instead, he tries to awaken guilt in her by threatening to return to the misery of Hell. He paints a picture of himself back in the "cold and the gloom, the lonely, lonely streets." And when she says, "Don't talk like that," he seizes on what he thinks is her grief and guilt:

> Ah, you can't bear it. . . . You must be sheltered. Grim realities must be kept out of your sight. You who can be happy without me. . . . You say, don't. Don't tell you. Don't make you unhappy.

But Sarah quickly corrects him. She isn't telling him to stop because she can't handle the grief. She is telling him to stop for his own sake. And then she describes Frank's besetting sin, the sin that he must turn away from if he is to be saved.

> [Stop] using pity, other people's pity, in the wrong way. We have all done it a bit on earth, you know. Pity was meant to be a spur that drives joy to help misery. But it can be used the wrong way round. It can be used for a kind of

> blackmailing. Those who choose misery can hold joy up to ransom, by pity.
>
> You see, I know now. Even as a child you did it. Instead of saying you were sorry, you went and sulked in the attic . . . because you knew that sooner or later one of your sisters would say, "I can't bear to think of him sitting up there alone, crying." You used their pity to blackmail them, and they gave in in the end. And afterwards, when we were married . . . oh, it doesn't matter, if only you will stop it.[13]

Sarah's joy is now invulnerable to Frank's manipulations. Her love and joy are no longer at the mercy of his frowns and sighs. He can no longer hurt her, because she is in Love, and she cannot love a lie. In the end, Frank refuses to come out of his sulky selfishness and vanishes back to the Grey Town.

Weaponized Pity and True Compassion

Now, Lewis knew that his description of the invulnerability of joy would be shocking to his readers. Many will have the same question that the narrator in the story does, when he asks his guide, George MacDonald, "Is it really tolerable that she should be untouched by his misery, even his self-made misery?"

MacDonald presses through the apparent compassion and mercy of this question to point out the underlying reality. What lies beneath Frank's desire for Sarah to be

13. Lewis, *The Great Divorce*, 131–132.

touched by his misery is "the demand of the loveless and the self-imprisoned that they should be allowed to blackmail the universe: that till they consent to be happy (on their own terms) no one else shall taste joy: that theirs should be the final power; that hell should be able to veto heaven."[14]

And then the narrator asks the question that is central for us: "Dare one say that pity [compassion] should ever die?" MacDonald wisely says that we must distinguish between the action of pity and the passion of pity. The passion of pity is simply "an ache." It leads men to concede what should not be conceded. Under its influence, we surrender the truth out of misguided compassion for the hurting; we flatter others rather than speak the truth. As we saw earlier in Pam's interaction with Reginald, pity and compassion can be wielded as a weapon against good-hearted people.

On the other hand, the action of pity, or true compassion, is a weapon for the sons of light. It descends from the highest to the lowest place, no matter the cost. It causes transformation, bringing light into the darkness. And significantly, it refuses to submit to the tyranny of evil, no matter how many cunning tears Hell cries. True compassion will not lie—it will not call blue yellow to please those who insist on keeping their jaundice. It will not turn a garden into a dung heap because some people can't abide the smell of roses.

But even with this distinction in hand, readers will have more questions. Isn't Lewis commending heartlessness? As

14. Lewis, *The Great Divorce*, 135.

the narrator asks MacDonald after witnessing Pam and Reginald's conversation, "But could one dare—could one have the face—to go to a bereaved mother, in her misery—when one's not bereaved oneself?" MacDonald's response is crucial:

> No, no, son, that's no office of yours. You're not a good enough man for that. When your own heart's been broken it will be time for you to think of talking. But someone must say in general what's been unsaid among you this many a year: that love, as mortals understand the word, isn't enough. Every natural love will rise again and live forever in this country: but none will rise again until it has been buried.[15]

This is what Lewis is doing: attempting to say in general what many are afraid to say at all. But it's cruel not to say it, and the absence of such truth-telling is "why sorrows that used to purify now only fester." And then MacDonald insists on the same truth that we saw in *The Four Loves*.

> But you and I must be clear. There is but one good; that is God. Everything else is good when it looks to him and bad when it turns from him. And the higher and mightier it is in the natural order, the more demoniac it will be if it rebels. It's not out of bad mice or bad fleas you make demons, but out of bad archangels.[16]

15. Lewis, *The Great Divorce*, 105–106.
16. Lewis, *The Great Divorce*, 106.

In other words, love—even love for the hurting and broken—becomes a demon the moment that it becomes a god.

Applying Lewis's Insights

With these stories before us, how should we then live? How do we face the dangerous passion of pity? First, we must start with ourselves. We must repent of the Sulks. We must refuse to wield our afflictions as tools of manipulation. We must not throw pity parties. In short, we must not be like Frank.

Of course, this doesn't mean that we smother our pain and sorrow. Elsewhere, I've written about the need to grieve losses the way that the saints in Scripture do.[17] Think of David pouring out his heart to the Lord in the psalms. Or Job weeping in sackcloth and ashes over the death of his children. Or Mary, Martha, and Jesus at the tomb of Lazarus. There are good and godly ways to suffer and feel the burden of this broken and sinful world.

But it's easy to magnify our inconveniences in order to elicit sympathy from those who love us, to make martyrs out of ourselves and send our loved ones on a guilt trip. The Sulks are not only a danger for children. In fact, if anything, children are more honest about their attempts to manipulate. Ask a child if he is throwing a pity party, and he's likely to say "Yes." Ask an adult the same question,

17. Joe Rigney, *Strangely Bright: Can You Love God and Enjoy This World?*, 2nd ed. (Moscow, ID: Canon Press, 2024), chapter 6.

and you're likely to hear a cluster of denials, excuses, and rationalizations.

Second, we might consider the way that we wield the suffering of others in the same manner. Compassion is a great and glorious good, a spur to the joyful to help those who are suffering. But the line between spurring the joyful to help misery and using the misery of others to steer the merciful is not always easy to see. The tyrannical mother did not recognize her tyranny. From the inside, her mother-love was holy, righteous, and good.

Nor do we always recognize when our compassion ceases to be compassion and instead becomes a subtle tool of emotional blackmail. But if Lewis is right that the highest and best things become demoniac when they begin to be gods, then we ought to be aware that compassion—which is one of the highest and best things—can also fall into this trap. In our zeal to help the hurting, we can at times overthrow other virtues, such as charity, honesty, and justice. And, of course, *The Great Divorce* teaches us how to recognize the tricks of emotional saboteurs. Lewis's book holds up a mirror to our own relationships, so that we learn to resist the pity parties and guilt trips that others use to steer us.

Dethroning the Passion of Pity

However, I think that the best application of Lewis's insights comes from the Solid Spirits in his story. They are full of love; indeed they are in Love himself. Compassion—what

Lewis calls the action of pity—flows from them like streams of water from an inexhaustible fountain. At the same time, because they are perfected in glory, they are beyond sorrow and pain. As a result, it's necessary for us to bring Lewis's heavenly picture down to earth, to apply the heavenly compassion in our pilgrim condition. What might this look like?

Faithful compassion leans into the suffering of others, weeping with those who weep, genuinely joining the sorrowful in their grief, and then, when the time is right, taking action to relieve the pain. But while compassion will leap from the heights of joy to the depths of sorrow in order to bring healing, even at great cost to itself, it will refuse to be steered by the manipulations of the afflicted. True compassion always reserves the right not to blaspheme.

Like Job, compassion can absorb the grief-driven accusations of a bereaved mother and refuse to curse God and die (Job 2:9–10). It refuses to concede what should not be conceded, even in the face of great human suffering. It refuses to flatter under the pressure of pity. Instead, it insists on speaking the truth (or at least clinging to the truth, if wisdom directs that it's not yet time to speak). Compassion is willing to be called "heartless" in its pursuit of the true and lasting good of the afflicted. True compassion is stable and calm, which gives it the paradoxical ability to move toward the hurting without being swallowed by their grief.

Compassion ceases to be a demon when it ceases to be a god, and compassion becomes itself, in all of its glory, when it revels in the fact that God is God, merciful and gracious and abounding in steadfast love.

3
THE SINS OF EMPATHS

IN THE LAST CHAPTER, WE NOTED THE way that weaponized pity or empathy can be used to manipulate others. In this chapter, we'll see what emotional blackmail does to a community when it's left unchecked. The effects may not be what you expect. Despite the appearance of love and mercy that empathy puts on, I want to argue that a community in the grip of empathy winds up being characterized by three traits: cowardice, indifference, and cruelty.

While Chesterton and Lewis warned us about the dangers of untruthful pity, it is Edwin Friedman who was most responsible for exposing the destructive capacity of empathy in the modern world, especially in relation to social systems and leadership.

In his book *A Failure of Nerve*, Friedman identifies empathy as a liability for leaders, especially when elevated as the premier virtue. According to Friedman, while it's essential for leaders to feel for others, care for others, identify with others, respond to others, and share the pain of others, in the modern context, empathy is often "a disguise for anxiety . . . and a power tool in the hands of the sensitive."[1]

For Friedman, the issue is not *whether* we should care for those who are hurting; he was, after all, a marriage and family therapist. The issue is whether the sensitivities and concerns of the most reactive and least mature members of a community (family, church, business, etc.) should be allowed to set the agenda.

Friedman writes, "I have consistently found the introduction of the subject of 'empathy' into family, institutional, and community meetings to be reflective of, as well as an effort to induce, a failure of nerve among its leadership."[2] Why then is empathy so prominent in the modern world?

1. Friedman, *A Failure of Nerve*, 133.
2. Friedman, *A Failure of Nerve*, 133.

> Empathy, "to feel in" . . . was intended to be an advance over old-fashioned concepts such as sympathy or compassion, which mean only "to feel or to suffer with." . . . I believe that the increasing popularity of empathy over the past few decades is symptomatic of the herding/togetherness force characteristic of an anxious society.[3]

Elsewhere, he argues, "[O]ur focus on empathy is one of the major factors that has everybody stuck . . . The concept of empathy has wound up encouraging everyone to lose their own boundaries, so it works against the very self-regulation that is necessary for it to be employed objectively."[4]

In one of his more provocative analogies, Friedman argued that the elevation of empathy empowered what he calls "viral members" of a community—that is, members who lack self-definition and self-regulation and are therefore perpetually invading the space of others.[5] Such people are "easily hurt injustice collectors, slow healers who are given to victim attitudes." They "tend to idolize their leaders until their unrealistic expectations fail, whereupon they are quick to crucify their 'gods.'" They often get stuck in "linear, black-and-white formulations" and "unconditional with-us-or-against-us attitudes" that cannot tolerate difference or dissent. They fixate on "procedure and rituals" and, in their myopia, are unable to see the emotional processes

3. Friedman, *A Failure of Nerve*, 136.
4. Edwin H. Friedman, "Empathy Defeats Therapy," in *The Myth of the Shiksa and Other Essays*, (New York: Church Publishing Incorporated, 2008), 119.
5. Friedman, *A Failure of Nerve*, 154–155.

that are spawning the issues. They "thrive in the darkness of conspiracy," and manifest three characteristics: "a high degree of reactivity, a narrow range of responses, and of course they are always serious—deadly serious." They are "unforgivingly relentless and invulnerable to insight" and are easily "stampeded and panicked into group-think, thus fusing with others like them into an undifferentiated mass." And crucial for our purposes, they thrive in highly empathetic environments, manipulating the compassion of the community while avoiding responsibility for their own emotions and behavior.

In another essay, Friedman offers a fictionalized interview with the first family counselor in history—namely, the Devil. The interviewer is in normal text, and the Devil is in italics:

> *Political rhetoric encourages everyone to lower their threshold for pain. It supports a quick-fix attitude. Haven't you ever noticed that in any counseling session or at any community meeting the persons most apt to mention "trust," "sensitivity," "confidentiality," "togetherness," and "consensus" are always the ones who want others to adapt to them?*
>
> These concepts have great communal potential.
>
> *They used to, but through the word "empathy" I have succeeded in turning them into abuses of power.*
>
> You're taking credit for empathy?
>
> *It's probably the most regressive concept I have ever employed.*
>
> Regressive? It's the foundation of many modern approaches to relationships.

> *But it makes feelings more important than boundaries. It's a very late concept, you know . . . Came into English about 1922 actually. At first I didn't pay too much attention to it, but then I began to realize that by getting everyone to substitute empathy for compassion—feeling* in *supposedly being better than feeling* with—*I saw that I could generally frustrate the Creator's plan for an evolving response to challenge because everyone would stay focused on one another instead of themselves.*[6]

In warning about empathy, Friedman is not commending callousness, apathy, or narcissism. Instead, he is insisting that we increase our threshold for one another's pain so that we are able to challenge them to take responsibility for their own emotional well-being. Such differentiation and self-regulation on our part enables us to then rightly feel for others, care for others, identify with others, and respond to others.[7]

Friedman's emphasis on differentiation and the danger of empathy has been expanded by other family systems thinkers. Here is Steve Cuss in a recent book on leadership anxiety:

> Differentiation is the ability to be fully yourself while being fully connected to people. It is gaining clarity on where "I" ends and the "other" begins. A differentiated person allows space between herself and another, even when that other person is highly anxious or asking for

6. Friedman, "An Interview with the First Family Counselor," in *The Myth of the Shiksa*, 27.
7. Friedman, *A Failure of Nerve*, 136–137.

> rescue. A differentiated leader is clear on her own values and convictions and is not easily swayed from them.
>
> The opposites on either side of differentiation are enmeshment and detachment. An enmeshed leader is unable to hold any space between himself and the other. If the other is struggling, the enmeshed leader gets pulled into it. The detached leader holds too much space between himself and the other. There is so much space the leader does not care for the other. An enmeshed leader struggles with codependency but calls it empathy. The detached leader struggles with indifference and thinks it is healthy. In contrast, a differentiated leader is fully present, but fully intact, with space between where he or she ends and the other begins.[8]

What Cuss calls detachment, I call apathy. And, like Friedman before him, Cuss connects empathy to enmeshment, or fusion.

Even in the 90s, Friedman was aware that criticizing empathy would be shocking to his audience. Empathy, he wrote, has "achieved such an inviolable, holy status in the thinking of some that to even question its value will be considered as irreverent, if not sacrilegious."[9] At the same time, Friedman asserts that the emotional fusion that lurks beneath modern appeals to empathy "is far more destructive than lack of concern or understanding."[10]

8. Steve Cuss, *Managing Leadership Anxiety: Yours and Theirs* (Nashville: Thomas Nelson, 2019), 119.

9. Friedman, *A Failure of Nerve*, 136.

10. Friedman, "Empathy Defeats Therapy," in *The Myth of the Shiksa,* 119.

Empathy and Cowardice

Why is untethered empathy so destructive? In the last chapter, we noted the way that weaponized pity or empathy can be used to manipulate others. At the extreme end, we can think of the way that the transgender movement uses the prospect of suicide to manipulate parents into "affirming" their child's "gender identity." "Would you rather have a dead son or a live daughter?" This is a hostage situation, filled with manipulation. John Piper calls this "emotional blackmail."

> Emotional blackmail happens when a person equates his or her emotional pain with another person's failure to love. They aren't the same. A person may love well and the beloved still feel hurt, and use the hurt to blackmail the lover into admitting guilt he or she does not have. Emotional blackmail says, "If I feel hurt by you, you are guilty." There is no defense. The hurt person has become God. His emotion has become judge and jury. Truth does not matter. All that matters is the sovereign suffering of the aggrieved. It is beyond question. This emotional device is a great evil. I have seen it often in my three decades of ministry, and I am eager to defend people who are being wrongly indicted by it.[11]

When these dynamics are present, empathy often leads to cowardice, to an unwillingness to say (even in a general way) anything that might cause distress to others—and

11. Justin Taylor, "Tozer's Contradiction and His Approach to Piety," *Between Two Worlds*, June 9, 2008, https://www.thegospelcoalition.org/blogs/justin-taylor/tozers-contradiction-and-his-approach_08/.

particularly to those who have been hurt. Out of a good and sincere desire to protect victims of trauma and abuse, certain topics and truths are ruled out of bounds. They must not be discussed (or they must be discussed only with layers upon layers of qualifications) because of the possibility that the discussion might cause further distress to those who have been hurt.

In the grip of empathy, we're unable to distinguish between the *distress* of others and *harm* to others. And out of a good desire to avoid causing harm, we commit to not saying or doing anything that might cause distress. In such an environment, our ability to speak the truth contracts and constricts (sometimes under pressure from highly empathetic people), and as Lewis said, "sorrows that used to purify now only fester."[12]

Lest we think that empathy is a danger only when faced with genuine suffering and hardship, consider the ways that abusers manipulate the feelings of their victims. Having committed some grievous sin, they say, "Don't tell anyone. If they found out, I'd be in so much trouble." This is a direct manipulation of the empathy of a victim.

And the manipulation doesn't stop there. Abusers very often play on the soft-heartedness of churches and communities in order to evade responsibility for their actions. They redirect attention away from the suffering of actual victims to their own suffering as perpetrators, counting on

12. Lewis, *The Great Divorce*, 106.

our empathetic emotion-sharing to suspend our rational judgment about what should be done.

In such cases, churches don't suffer from a lack of empathy so much as a radically misplaced empathy. Ensuring that our feelings are directed in the right place requires that we maintain the appropriate emotional boundaries so that we can think clearly and rightly about our particular situation. In other words, compassion, with its insistence on self-differentiation and concern for long-term good, is what is needed.

Empathy and Indifference

The possibility of misplaced empathy highlights another danger—selective empathy. Paul Bloom, a cognitive neuroscientist and author of *Against Empathy: The Case for Rational Compassion*, describes what might be called empathetic myopia.[13] Bloom notes that, because we are finite and can feel the feelings of only a limited number of people, empathy is of necessity highly selective. We simply can't empathize with everybody. Empathy, therefore, behaves like a spotlight, illuminating the suffering and feelings of particular people or groups and not others. This empathetic tunnel vision creates competing empathies: some people identify with the suffering of one group, and others identify with the suffering of another group. As a result of these competing empathies, each side often

13. Paul Bloom, *Against Empathy: The Case for Rational Compassion* (New York: Ecco, 2016).

struggles to see the big picture. We fail to maintain an appropriate measure of objectivity.

The politics of abortion is shot through with this sort of empathetic myopia. Abortion advocates frequently leverage empathy for poor and endangered women to sanction the murder of unborn children. For example, a 2023 political ad in the Kentucky governor's race featured a rape victim who looked into the camera and said the following:

> I was raped by my stepfather after years of sexual abuse. I was twelve. Anyone who believes that there should be no exceptions for rape and incest could never understand what it's like to stand in my shoes. This is to you, Daniel Cameron. To tell a twelve-year-old girl she must have the baby of her stepfather who raped her is unthinkable. I'm speaking out because women and girls need to have options. Daniel Cameron would give us none.[14]

The ad is fundamentally an appeal to the electorate's compassion: "Imagine this was you, or your daughter." And of course, compassion is manifestly called for. Great evil was done to this young woman. But the great evil that has been done to this young woman is being used to disguise the great evil that will be done to the innocent child. In the ad, the euphemism "options" means "murder." This sort of obfuscation is made possible by empathy. The rape

14. Medium Buying (@MediumBuying), 2023, "The Andy Beshear campaign is up on TV with this spot," X, September 20, 2023, 5:53 A.M., https://x.com/MediumBuying/status/1704479015992447432.

victim is visible and, therefore, a suitable object of our pity. The unborn child is not, and can therefore be dispensed with. The pro-life movement has sought (with some success) to combat this empathetic myopia with pictures of fetal body parts and videos of ultrasounds. These images make the unborn child an object of compassion in the face of the dehumanizing rhetoric of the culture of Death. Indeed, comparing the two sorts of appeal demonstrates the difference between untethered empathy and biblical compassion. The latter appeal to pathos is designed to reveal and underscore what is true and good (the full humanity of the unborn child), whereas the former is designed specifically to obscure it.

Indifference to the unborn child is just one example of the way that empathy is selective and myopic. When unmoored from reason and justice, it blinds us so that we're unable to feel compassion for those who are outside the range of vision set by empathy.

Empathy and Cruelty

However, the selectivity of empathy often leads to more than blindness; it frequently leads to brazen malice and cruelty. As Bloom says, "[W]hen some people think about empathy, they think about kindness. I think about war."[15] In the same vein, Hannah Arendt has written, "[P]ity,

15. Jonah Goldberg, "Is Empathy a Distraction in Health-Care Debate?" *The Baltimore Sun*, May 08, 2017, https://www.baltimoresun.com/opinion/op-ed/bal-jonah-goldberg-is-empathy-a-distraction-in-health-care-debate-20170505-story.html.

taken as the spring of virtue, has proved to possess a greater capacity for cruelty than cruelty itself."[16]

The cruelty of empathy came home to me during COVID, when David French criticized my writings on empathy in an article entitled "The American Crisis of Selective Empathy."[17] French was prompted to engage by examples of "death shaming" toward those who died from COVID after refusing to take the vaccine. French was understandably shocked by the callousness and schadenfreude of Americans toward those who chose to forego vaccination. According to French, this callousness was the result of our empathy crisis. In particular, he highlighted the tribalism and partisanship that warp our empathy, leading us to direct it toward those in our political, cultural, ethnic, or religious tribe (and not toward those who are different from us). Engaging with my writings, he argued that our problem is not *excessive* empathy but *selective* empathy.

But what French fails to reckon with is that our empathy is selective ***precisely because*** it is excessive. Again, to summarize Bloom, we find it easy to demonize those that we don't feel empathy for. Thus, intense empathy for our in-group often goes hand in hand with intense anger (and even hatred) for our out-group. We turn our opponents into devils because they're easier to hate. Thus, a recent spate of articles has noted that an increase in empathy, far from

16. Hannah Arendt, *On Revolution* (London: Penguin Books, 1990), 89.

17. David French, "The American Crisis of Selective Empathy," *The Dispatch*, September 12, 2021, https://thedispatch.com/newsletter/frenchpress/the-american-crisis-of-selective/?triedSigningIn=true.

building connection, seems to be joined with increased polarization and tribalism.[18] One peer-reviewed study concluded that "empathic concern does not reduce partisan animosity in the electorate and in some respects even exacerbates it."[19] The study found that "high-empathy people view the out group more unfavorably (relative to their own group) than low-empathy people; and that they may even take more delight in the suffering of some out-group members."[20]

To put a point on this: how many of the COVID-death-shamers would describe themselves as highly empathetic people in general? My guess is that almost all of them would. And they aren't wrong.

Seventy years ago, C.S. Lewis identified the reduction of all virtues to kindness as the source of this cruelty.

> Are we not really an increasingly cruel age? Perhaps we are: but I think we have become so in the attempt to reduce all virtues to kindness. For Plato rightly taught that virtue is one. You cannot be kind unless you have all the other virtues. If, being cowardly, conceited and slothful, you

18. Hanna Rosin, "The End of Empathy," *National Public Radio*, April 15, 2019, https://www.npr.org/2019/04/15/712249664/the-end-of-empathy; Scott Barry Kaufman, "Can Empathic Concern Actually Increase Political Polarization?" *Scientific American*, November 6, 2019, https://blogs.scientificamerican.com/beautiful-minds/can-empathic-concern-actually-increase-political-polarization/; Robert Wright, "Empathy Is Tearing Us Apart," *Wired*, November 9, 2019, https://www.wired.com/story/empathy-is-tearing-us-apart/.
19. Wright, "Empathy Is Tearing Us Apart."
20. Wright, "Empathy Is Tearing Us Apart."

> have never yet done a fellow creature great mischief, that is only because your neighbour's welfare has not yet happened to conflict with your safety, self-approval, or ease. Every vice leads to cruelty.[21]

Lewis then, like Chesterton before him, applies this principle explicitly to pity.

> Even a good emotion, pity, if not controlled by charity and justice, leads through anger to cruelty. Most atrocities are stimulated by accounts of the enemy's atrocities; and pity for the oppressed classes, when separated from the moral law as a whole, leads by a very natural process to the unremitting brutalities of a reign of terror.[22]

Pity, when untethered from charity, justice, and the moral law, leads through anger to cruelty. One only has to look at various conflicts around the world to see the ease with which pity for one's tribe leads to malice and hatred for another. Elsewhere, Lewis describes the same phenomenon in relation to mercy, accenting the need for mercy to be tethered to justice.

> Mercy, detached from Justice, grows unmerciful. That is the important paradox. As there are plants which will flourish only in mountain soil, so it appears that Mercy will flower only when it grows in the crannies of the

21. C.S. Lewis, *The Problem of Pain* (New York: HarperOne, 2001), 59.
22. Lewis, *The Problem of Pain*, 59.

> rock of Justice: transplanted to the marshlands of mere Humanitarianism, it becomes a man-eating weed, all the more dangerous because it is still called by the same name as the mountain variety.[23]

As with mercy, so with empathy. Untethered from justice and the moral law and planted in the sentimental marshlands of humanitarianism (or critical theory), empathy becomes a man-eating weed, devouring families, relationships, even churches and ministries. The subject of the next chapter is how it has done just that.

23. C.S. Lewis, *God in the Dock*, ed. Walter Hooper (New York: HarperOne, 1994), 326–327.

4
LIFE UNDER THE PROGRESSIVE GAZE

OVER THE LAST DECADE OR SO, AMERICAN society has endured a series of conflicts surrounding race, sexuality, abuse, and LGBTQ+. In each of these conflicts, the progressives have become popularly known as "woke." Conflicts over wokeness in American society spilled over into the church, with particular events—Ferguson, *Obergefell*, the #MeToo movement, the election(s) of Donald Trump, the rise of Black Lives Matter, COVID, and the death of George Floyd—acting as flashpoints.

One of my basic contentions is that a common denominator in the conflicts surrounding all things "woke" is untethered empathy. Others have written about the ideological dimension of these conflicts, exploring their roots in cultural Marxism and critical theory. But I believe an ideological evaluation of wokeness is insufficient. Persuasion is a matter of logos (appeals to reason and facts), pathos (appeals to emotion), and ethos (appeals to credibility). If we want to understand how the woke rot penetrated so deeply into society and the church, we must see how debate and discussion about the ideas were smothered by excessive pathos and ethos, by untethered empathy and appeals to credibility.

The Quest for Credibility

To set the stage, we'll begin with Aaron Renn's Three Worlds Framework. It will help us to pinpoint where the church lost the plot. Over the last few years, Renn's framework has become a common tool for describing evangelicalism's relationship to American culture. Here is Renn's succinct summary.

> Within the story of American secularization, there have been three distinct stages:
>
> Positive World (Pre-1994): Society at large retains a mostly *positive* view of Christianity. To be known as a good, churchgoing man remains part of being an upstanding citizen. Publicly being a Christian is a status-enhancer.

Christian moral norms are the basic moral norms of society and violating them can bring negative consequences.

Neutral World (1994–2014): Society takes a *neutral* stance toward Christianity. Christianity no longer has privileged status but is not disfavored. Being publicly known as a Christian has neither a positive nor a negative impact on one's social status. Christianity is a valid option within a pluralistic public square. Christian moral norms retain some residual effect.

Negative World (2014–Present): Society has come to have a *negative* view of Christianity. Being known as a Christian is a social negative, particularly in the elite domains of society. Christian morality is expressly repudiated and seen as a threat to the public good and the new public moral order. Subscribing to Christian moral views or violating the secular moral order brings negative consequences.[1]

Renn identifies distinct ministry strategies that Christians used in Positive and Neutral World. Positive World strategies included culture war and seeker sensitivity. The Neutral World strategy was cultural engagement. It was in Neutral World that empathy began to weaken the church's foundation.

For our purposes, a few features of Renn's treatment of Neutral World stand out. First, culture-engagers placed a particular emphasis on cities. The culture that they sought

1. Aaron M. Renn, "The Three Worlds of Evangelicalism," First Things, February 2022, https://firstthings.com/article/2022/02/the-three-worlds-of-evangelicalism

to engage was urban, elite, and secular. As a result, culture-engagers sought to maintain a seat at the pluralistic table for the sake of Christian witness. And in pursuit of that seat, culture-engagers consciously sought to differentiate themselves from the culture warriors of the religious right. The Moral Majority was out; the "Prophetic Minority" was in. This differentiation was centered on ministry posture: winsome (not hostile), compassionate (not harsh), and nuanced (not black-and-white). These virtues offered credibility, and in Neutral World, credibility was currency.

Now of course, God commends these virtues in the Bible. Paul tells us, "The Lord's servant must not be quarrelsome but kind to everyone, able to teach, patiently enduring evil, correcting his opponents with gentleness. God may perhaps grant them repentance leading to a knowledge of the truth, and they may come to their senses and escape from the snare of the devil, after being captured by him to do his will" (2 Tim. 2:24–26). Kind, not quarrelsome. Patient, gentle, and aiming at persuading one's opponents. Throughout the New Testament, we see Paul seeking to remove unnecessary barriers to the Christian faith, culturally adapting to his audience in order that by any means possible he might save some (1 Cor. 9:19–22). And the book of Proverbs commends wisdom and discernment when engaging with complex issues in a fallen world.

But the pursuit of these virtues had an unintended side effect. The quest for credibility in urban, elite contexts and the desire to differentiate themselves from the culture warriors meant that culture-engagers came to live their lives and conduct their ministries under the progressive gaze.

The Progressive Gaze

The progressive gaze is my modification of the concept of "the white gaze." Popularized by novelist Toni Morrison, "the white gaze" has to do with one's default reader or observer, the idealized audience for which someone writes and speaks. Black authors (Morrison claimed) feel constrained to adapt to the assumptions of white readers. In other words, the default assumptions of white readers are taken to be normative. As the entry in Wikipedia puts it, "[V]arious authors of color describe it as a voice in their heads that reminds them that their writing, characters, and plot choices are going to be judged by white readers, and that the reader or viewer, by default, is white."[2]

Morrison once asked, "What happens to the writerly imagination of a black author who is at some level always conscious of representing one's race to, or in spite of, a race of readers that understands itself to be 'universal' or race-free?"[3] The unspoken implication, of course, is that the

2. "White Gaze," Wikipedia, last modified December 2, 2024, https://en.wikipedia.org/wiki/White_gaze#:~:text=The%20white%20gaze%20is%20the,white%20reader%20or%20observer's%20reaction.

3. LJ Alonge, "Writing Past the White Gaze as a Black Author," Code Switch, March 4, 2017, https://www.npr.org/sections/codeswitch/2017/03/04/515790514/writing-past-the-white-gaze-as-a-black-author.

imagination is stunted, strangled, and smothered beneath such pressure.

The progressive gaze simply identifies a different audience. Under the progressive gaze, the default unbeliever, before whom we live and move and have our being, is presumed to be urban, liberal, and progressive—and thus we write and speak in such a way that our words (we think) will have maximum persuasive power to them. We write so as to make the Christian faith comprehensible to the progressive, attempting insofar as we can to validate their concerns and share their sensitivities in hopes of winning them to the gospel. You know you're under the influence of the progressive gaze when someone says, "Remember: the world is watching," and "the world" is presumed to be coastal elites who inhabit urban centers (as opposed to the coal miner in the red hat who hasn't been to church since he was eight).

In Neutral World, many Christians came to have an imaginary progressive in their head (or on their shoulder), and this imaginary progressive began to shape their rhetoric, orientation, and framing of various issues. Over time, everyone began to assume that it was progressive sensitivities that Christians must take into account, progressive concerns that we must speak to, progressive hopes that we must show the gospel subversively fulfilling, progressive hostilities that we must share, and progressive enemies that we must denounce. In sum, in Neutral World, many evangelical Christians sought to maintain a seat at the pluralistic table by pursuing credibility in the eyes of urban progressives, and thus they came to live beneath the progressive gaze. The result? When Neutral World gave way to Negative World, we weren't ready.

The Shift to Negative World

As the pluralistic public square gave way to a new public civil religion, progressives began to use this obsession with credibility to steer evangelicals, especially evangelical leaders. For our purposes, I'll simply sketch the outlines of the steering.[4]

Under the progressive gaze, progressive values and concerns were normalized and taken to be the default operating system for society. Mainline Christian denominations baptized these progressive values, loosely attaching Bible verses to them (while studiously ignoring or denying the rest of the biblical witness).

These default progressive values included the oppressor-oppressed framework derived from critical theory, as well as the intersectionality that piles up oppression to create a hierarchy of victims. Living under the progressive gaze, Christian churches implicitly adopted the progressive victimhood hierarchy, identifying minorities (especially African Americans), immigrants, women, and the LBGTQ+

4. For a more detailed account of how progressive activists laundered their leftist agenda into churches and Christian ministries, see Megan Basham, *Shepherds for Sale: How Evangelical Leaders Traded the Truth for a Leftist Agenda* (New York: Broadside Books, 2024). Basham identifies high-profile examples of compromise, drift, and hijacking in relation to climate change, immigration, abortion, COVID, race, and sexuality.

community as oppressed. At this point, Christian compassion, which was degenerating into empathy, kicked in, and under the banner of social justice, Christians became Advocates and Activists, seeking to rectify past and present wrongs and build "credibility" for the gospel. Certain events (such as the shooting of Michael Brown or the death of George Floyd) became totems for narratives of oppression and victimhood, testifying to the abiding injustices in our culture, and thereby afforded opportunities to virtue signal under the progressive gaze.

Given America's history, racism was particularly potent as the leading edge of the progressive gaze. Churches started book clubs and Sunday school classes that reinforced the progressive gaze, acquainting their congregations with concepts like anti-racism and white fragility. Accusations of misogyny and sexism in the church were likewise animating forces, again awakening compassion and inspiring advocates for various kinds of reform. And it's important to stress that, in some cases, real victims of real evil were in view, and Christians were rightly moved by sincere compassion and a desire to rectify wrongs. At the same time, many of the books circulating offered skewed narratives based on specious statistics (such as "1 in 4 women are the victims of sexual assault," or "Blacks are imprisoned at a disproportionate rate").[5] The statistics provided just enough of a veneer of truth to reinforce these

5. For analysis of the statistics on sexual assault, see Basham, *Shepherds for Sale*, 152–193. For the statistics concerning crime, consult Jeremy Carl, *The Unprotected Class: How Anti-White Racism Is Tearing America Apart* (Regnery, 2024).

narratives, narratives that were fundamentally motivated by empathy and the quest for credibility.

After the effectiveness of these initial movements, however, the definition of victimhood was expanded through language inflation and concept creep. Terms like "abuse" and "trauma" were enlarged to encompass a wider array of experiences. No longer did abuse refer to a pattern of physical or sexual violence; now criticism, rebuke, correction, and even disagreement could be regarded as abuse. No longer did trauma refer to physical damage, or even an event causing severe emotional distress outside the range of usual human experience. Instead, *any* emotional distress was regarded as harmful, and empathy demanded that Christians comfort, nurture, and accommodate the traumatized.[6] Christians came to implicitly adopt the subjective logic of victimhood—"I'm hurt, therefore, you sinned"—and thereby succumbed to the tyranny of the sensitive.

This story played out in hundreds of churches and ministries in various ways over the last decade. Through a mix of empathy, faux justice, and credibility, the world discovered a powerful steering wheel for the church, one that

6. For a helpful article summarizing language inflation and concept creep, see Andrew David Naselli, "Ten Resources That Have Helped Me Make Sense of Our Current Culture and How Christians Are Responding To It," *Eikon* 4, no. 1 (Spring 2022), 118–43. Naselli particularly highlights Greg Lukianoff and Jonathan Haidt, *The Coddling of the American Mind: How Good Intentions and Bad Ideas Are Setting up a Generation for Failure* (New York: Penguin, 2018); Bradley Campbell and Jason Manning, *The Rise of Victimhood Culture: Microaggressions, Safe Spaces, and the New Culture Wars* (Cham, Switzerland: Palgrave Macmillan, 2018); and Nick Haslam, "Concept Creep: Psychology's Expanding Concepts of Harm and Pathology," *Psychological Inquiry* 27, no. 1 (2016): 1–17.

progressive billionaires exploited to neutralize and co-opt God's people for their own purposes. In all of this, many Christians (and especially Christian leaders) had their eyes on three groups, all of whom reinforced the progressive gaze: Victims or oppressed groups (the objects of empathy), Advocates (the arbiters of justice), and other Respectable Christians (the purveyors of credibility). Let's look at each of them in turn.

The Victims

Churches have always had relational snarls. But in the last decade, many of these conflicts came to a head with church members accusing their pastors of spiritual and emotional abuse, to the bewilderment of many. And in some cases, there may have been real sin involved on the part of leaders. But in many cases, beneath the accusations was the empathetic logic of "I'm hurt, therefore, you sinned." A pastor who resisted such logic would undoubtedly be accused of deflection and denial. Any defense was tantamount to a confession of guilt.

In some of the more bewildering cases, members would leave a church on difficult but reasonable terms, with documentation to prove it, only to turn around a few years later and accuse their leaders of abuse. What happened? Under the influence of Advocates (see below), such members had re-narrated their stories in light of the prevailing ideology of victimhood. What they formerly regarded as conflict and disagreement was now abuse. Additionally, in certain cases, the new victimhood narrative covered over preexisting marital troubles. A husband and wife who had been at odds with each other for years found the marriage bond renewed by a shared enemy.

How did these former members explain the obvious shift in their original departure and the newer accusations? They often explained it through accusations of gaslighting, a form of psychological manipulation in which the abuser sows self-doubt and confusion in their victim's mind such that they question their perception of reality. Behavior that the church member had been taught was normal they "now realized" was psychological abuse. The difficulty with all such accusations was that the definition of abuse had been enlarged through concept creep, and the standard of judgment had been radically subjectivized. The feelings of the accuser were sufficient to condemn. The irony is that, in some cases, accusations of gaslighting were a form of projection, as leaders were gaslit by their "victims." "Did I actually cause them trauma? Am I an abuser?"

In a similar vein, consider a hypothetical discussion about racial reconciliation in the mid-2010s. Over the course of the conversation, it becomes increasingly unclear what kind of conversation you're having. One minute, it's a listening session, allowing minorities the chance to share their experiences. As a pastor, you have a category for that. There's a time to listen, to seek to understand what people have gone through. Perhaps to ask a question or two. But then the conversation moves to a discussion of what the church must do going forward. As a pastor, you also have a category for working with fellow Christians to come up with solutions to problems. And so as the discussion continues, you begin to ask different kinds of questions, to challenge assumptions, to give your own perspective, and so forth. Immediately, the tone shifts. The mood darkens. A rebuke is offered. "Why can't you just listen to our brothers and sisters tell their stories? Why do you have to insist on imposing your white perspective on everything?"

This is a subtle bait and switch, enabled by untethered empathy. Are you supposed to orient to someone as a *distressed sufferer* who just needs to be heard with compassion? Or as a *sober-minded co-laborer* working to make wise and biblical decisions in the pursuit of ethnic harmony?

The same dynamics often manifest in discussions of abuse. A meeting is called to hear from victims of domestic abuse. You listen with compassion as women tell stories of violence and assault, of manipulation and oppression. But then a proposal is made to form a task force to address the issue. You have questions. What will the scope of the task force be? Who will they report to? What kind of authority will they have? Again, the mood shifts. "Why are you opposing efforts to address abuse? Why are you not honoring victims and their stories?"

The net effect of these dynamics is to render certain subjects off-limits in the presence of victims, lest they be disrespected, triggered, or even re-traumatized. And yet to ask the Victims to step outside so you can talk frankly and clearly about the issues is clearly out of the question. The result is a kind of hostage situation. For example, in the conversation about race, suppose that someone brought up "white fragility," the notion that white people find the entire discussion about race so uncomfortable that they reactively shut down or blow up in the face of it. "Yes," you say, "white fragility is a real thing. I've seen it. But are we allowed to talk about black fragility? About the implicit threat of 'leaving loud' if we disagree with particular analyses or proposals?"

The Advocates

As noted above, the challenge of navigating these waters over the last couple decades was not limited to caring for Victims while attempting to make sober-minded decisions. The rise of Advocates further complicated the situation.

Many Advocates, no doubt, began with the best of intentions. Moved by compassion for the hurting, they set out to offer both comfort and justice to victims. However, excessive compassion coupled with intense zeal for justice opened the way for neglecting actual justice.

This was a particular danger in the case of Victims-Turned-Advocates. Imagine a victim of domestic abuse, someone who was genuinely oppressed, manipulated, and harmed by a wicked man. She eventually becomes an Advocate, starting a ministry to help other women. One of the fundamental temptations for her will be to read every story she hears in the light of her own, projecting her experience onto others'. This is how the language of abuse was inflated and the concept of trauma was enlarged. Normal marital challenges began to be regarded as abusive. A wider circle of "abuse" victims formed, and the pressure to accommodate them was intense. Victims-Turned-Advocates discovered that they were able to wield their credibility as survivors ("I've seen this a thousand times") and the empathy of the church in order to steamroll any opposition. And again, they sometimes did so with the best of intentions.

Powered by untethered empathy, churches became subject to a variety of hostage situations. Every disgruntled employee or congregant who left the church was welcomed with open arms by a cottage industry of books, conferences, and ministries dedicated to helping them re-narrate their stories, discover how they were abused, and become Advocates themselves. And again, in certain cases, there was no doubt sin (perhaps even grievous sin) on the part of leaders and churches. But many churches discovered that mere accusations were sufficient to convict them in the court of public opinion. Complex pastoral situations were now adjudicated, not in courts or in church meetings, but on social media. Words like "toxic" and "problematic" were tossed around with vague connotations of wrongdoing. A cloud of concern began to hover over the church and its leaders, with increasing demands for churches to open third-party investigations from approved "ministries." (One wonders if such ministries ever encountered a case of *false* accusations and vindicated the conduct and reputation of the accused.)

The Respectable

As the field of competitive victimhood expanded and the language of abuse was inflated beyond all recognition, "flopping" became common. We're all familiar with videos of soccer players who pretend to be assaulted by an opposing player in order to get the referee to call a penalty. The immature and reactive began to employ the same tactic in efforts to steer the church. The response from soft-hearted leaders often exacerbated the problem. If churches and leaders were steered by the Sensitive and their Advocates, they were frequently policed by the Respectable.

Some church leaders naively accepted the flop as genuine and put pressure on the accused to apologize. Others rightly identified the exaggerations of the accusers, but still applied the pressure. The goal was reconciliation through negotiated apologies: "I know that Susan overreacted and that you didn't mean what she said you meant. And she shouldn't have posted that inflammatory accusation online. Remember that she feels very deeply about these issues. She's taken the post down, and she's willing to apologize. But do you see how your words might have been taken? And can you apologize for the way that they came across and the hurt that they unintentionally caused?"

Now, of course, all Christians ought to be quick to seek forgiveness when they've wronged others. We ought to extend sincere apologies, with no hedging or qualifications. And this is true even when the lion's share of the blame falls on the other person. Taking responsibility for your contribution and acknowledging your sin (however small) is always required. But seeking forgiveness for real sins is different from apologizing for exaggerated "sins" in response to overreactions. Similarly, it is good and right to offer clarifications when someone is confused by something you've said. But offering clarifications is different from asking for forgiveness to appease those determined to misconstrue your words. Under the progressive gaze, soft-hearted, reasonable Christians replaced peacemaking with peace-mongering.

But negotiated apologies weren't the only steering wheel employed by the Respectable. Their acquiescence to the demands of Advocates (and the pressure they put on others to join them) was often fueled by fear of public accusations. In some cases, this meant that decent men put reactive people in charge of addressing volatile issues because "they clearly care about this issue." But such reasons were often simply rationalizations of the true reason, which was the fear that Victims or their Advocates would accuse them of enabling abuse or coddling abusers.

In other cases, Respectable leaders were steered by concern for their reputation (and then sought to steer others). Of course, Christian leaders ought to have a good reputation with outsiders (1 Tim. 3:7). This means that a man's unbelieving neighbor, who knows and interacts with him personally, ought to vouch for his character, even while rejecting the faith. "I don't embrace Bill's religion, but he coached my son in Little League and did a great job with the boys." However, we must remember that Paul wrote about the importance of a good reputation from prison, and, according to the Pharisees and priests, Jesus was a drunkard, a glutton, and a blasphemer. Good reputation indeed. Under the progressive gaze, worldly apostles (and their "Christian" fellow travelers) attacked faithful men in order to cast a fog of concern over them, and then relied on Respectables to police and distance themselves from them in the name of their "reputation."

Another common tactic involved reducing biblical truths to platitudes, and then using those platitudes to overcome resistance to particular progressive political or cultural priorities. "Love your neighbor; therefore, get vaccinated." "The world is watching; therefore, we must address this alleged abuse crisis in our denomination." "People are made in God's image; therefore, we must embrace amnesty and other progressive immigration policies."

Of course, there is no issue with drawing particular moral conclusions from a theological truth. Perhaps there are arguments to connect the premise to the conclusion. The issue is that often such arguments were not even attempted. Instead, when someone resisted the progressive *conclusion*, they were accused of rejecting the theological *principle*. The slogans became a steering wheel: "Adopt this particular approach to this issue, or you're a fundamentalist, a conspiracy theorist, a racist, or just a plain-old, bad Christian."

One set of slogans proved especially effective in blunting conservative Christian resistance to progressive cultural conquest: "Neither Republican nor Democrat"; "Neither the Donkey nor the Elephant"; "Neither Left nor Right but a Third Way"; "Prophetic, not Partisan." While these slogans arguably made sense in Positive World (when both parties still shared some of the same regard for the moral order of the universe and the differences largely revolved around wisely applying shared principles and wisely pursuing means to shared ends), in Negative World, they were simply neutering agents, resulting in what James Wood calls "culture-war quietism and political pietism."[7] This functional Anabaptism was driven by the desire to avoid the accusation of "politicizing the faith."

According to Wood, beneath this quietism and pietism lies a winsome, Third Way framework that views "politics through the lens of evangelism . . . Our political judgments and actions are filtered through how likely they will make our neighbors to receive the gospel message"[8] (and, under the progressive gaze, the relevant neighbors are assumed to be on the Left; no one is worried about validating the political concerns of rural whites concerned about mass immigration).

> In our intense cultural battles, conservative Christians are often reminded that because we must love our enemies and show the meekness of Christ, we should, therefore, avoid "culture-warring" or "politicizing the faith." Rather, we are told, we need to be "winsome" and find a way to

7. James R. Wood, "The Limits of Winsome Politics," *The American Conservative*, September 21, 2022, https://www.theamericanconservative.com/the-limits-of-winsome-politics/.

8. Wood, "Winsome Politics."

> transcend the divisions of our day. We are to lay down our rights, for the "world is watching." Any pursuit of power will, supposedly, discredit the church's public witness.
>
> Any attempt to "win" is characterized by our opponents as a mere power-grab and selfish pursuit of privileges. Critics claim that such pursuits of political victory reveal that we have made politics superior to our faith, that we instrumentalize the faith for partisan ends. They argue that, in so doing, we may win the world, but we definitely lose our souls. . . .
>
> The winsome framework inhibits our ability to act in accord with proper political prudence. This tricks us into thinking that we need to highlight the flaws in all sides with equal airtime or to put all issues on the same level, thus resulting in false moral equivalencies on issues and strategies, producing a crippling inability to recognize and publicly admit when there is moral asymmetry between contemporary sides and among the issues themselves.[9]

Under the progressive gaze, Third Way proponents were forced to balance the scales of evil by minimizing (or excusing) sins on the Left and exaggerating sins on the Right. This resulted in an unspoken slogan that went something like "Coddle left; punch right." "Winsome to the left; prophetic to the right." "Whisper to the left; thunder to the right."

One pastor told me that, after years of imbibing the "neither Left nor Right" framework, he came to realize that

9. Wood, "Winsome Politics."

there were only two political applications a conservative pastor was "allowed" to make publicly: either "The gospel is neither left nor right" or "The Left is actually correct about X." While he might have many more personal political convictions, those were the only ones that he could reasonably make publicly, lest he be accused of "politicizing the faith" or being "co-opted by right-wing partisanship." Even the *appearance* of partisanship was enough to lose one's "prophetic credibility."

What's more, leaders came to manifest what we might call misdirected boldness, what C.S. Lewis described as "running about with fire extinguishers whenever there is a flood."[10] Thus, many winsome pastors dedicated numerous sermons to smoking out (often imaginary) racists in their congregations, while soft feminism flourished under their leadership. They never dreamed of preaching boldly so as to "smoke out the feminists." This is because, under the progressive gaze, credibility and respectability are earned through appropriate empathy for designated groups, appropriate anger toward their "oppressors," and appropriate differentiation from other believers. "I thank you, God, that I'm not like those power-hungry culture warriors"; or again, "They will know that we are (respectable) Christians by our denunciations of the wrong kind of Christian." Those who resisted the false equivalencies and spoke with appropriate biblical clarity and boldness on *all* sins were policed as harsh, quarrelsome, partisan, and obsessed with political power.

10. C.S. Lewis, *The Screwtape Letters* (New York: HarperOne, 2001), 138.

Passions and the Progressive Gaze

In all of these cases, biblical virtues withered under the progressive gaze. Clarity degenerated into selective nuance and misdirected boldness, compassion degenerated into untethered empathy, kindness degenerated into winsome coddling, and a desire for a good reputation degenerated into man-pleasing and man-fearing. Candor and honesty were smothered beneath the progressive gaze. Christians began to censor themselves and became reluctant to challenge woke ideologies, to question specious proposals related to race, sex, and abuse, and to speak clearly about progressive sins. All of this was partly out of a desire to avoid alienating their target audience (progressives), partly out of fear of Advocates, and partly out of pressure from other respectable Christians.

Now of course there are other versions of this temptation, other "gazes" that we can live under. We might think of the female gaze, what some authors have referred to as "the Longhouse"—"the remarkable overcorrection of the last two generations toward social norms centering feminine needs and feminine methods for controlling, directing, and modeling behavior."[11] There are conservative, right-wing, and reactionary versions of the same emotional dynamics (though they are inevitably less potent because they lack the wider societal influence that enhances the progressive gaze). In fact, if we press into the psychological challenge of "the gaze" at all, we immediately realize that

11. Lom3z, "What Is the Longhouse?," First Things, February 16, 2023, https://www.firstthings.com/web-exclusives/2023/02/what-is-the-longhouse.

the Bible speaks directly to it. What we call "the gaze," the Bible calls simply fear of man or people-pleasing. It is a most subtle snare, twisting good things like friendship, partnership, and honoring leaders. For example, at Antioch, we're told that Peter compromised the gospel out of fear of the circumcision party (Gal. 2:12). He was living beneath the circumcised gaze. And then the rest of the Jewish Christians joined the hypocrisy because they were following Peter. In other words, they weren't fearing the world directly; instead, they were seeking the approval of a compromised apostle. Once the hypocritical compromise built up enough steam, even Barnabas went along with the crowd (Gal. 2:13).

Yes, the particular men whom we fear or people whom we seek to please may vary. But the temptation is universal.

The Bible places a sharp antithesis between seeking the approval of men and seeking the approval of God. As Paul says in Galatians 1:10, "For am I now seeking the approval of man, or of God? Or am I trying to please man? If I were still trying to please man, I would not be a servant of Christ." There it is, as simple as can be. We must choose: serve Christ or please men. Seek human approval or seek divine approval. To put it another way, the Scriptures insist that we remember a most basic fact, one so obvious that we are prone to forget it: "A man's ways are before the eyes of the Lord, and he ponders all his paths" (Prov. 5:21). All of us are "naked and exposed to the eyes of him to whom we must give account" (Heb. 4:13). In other words, all of us live and speak and act under the Divine Gaze.

The challenge comes in accepting and welcoming this fact—in calibrating our sensibilities, our framing of reality, our loves and our hates by what God says in his word, and not by any other human gaze (whether white, black, progressive, or otherwise).

But in American culture in the twenty-first century, it is the progressive gaze that poses the greatest threat to Christian faithfulness. Given the pervasiveness of progressive ideology in Big Government, Big Business, Big Tech, Big Education, Big Sports, and Big Media, the primary pressure on Christians is from the Left. And as this chapter indicates, the progressive gaze is fueled by passions—untethered empathy, the fear of man, and the desire for approval and respectability.

Passions, when unmoored, blind us and lead us astray, resulting in various degrees of self-deception. In many cases, we need not assume malicious intent on the part of those who are being steered or even those who attempt to steer others. In fact, making sense of the last decade demands that we stress the complexity of the motives involved in order to avoid simplistic narratives of "good guys" and "bad guys."

Picture a group of people standing next to one another with steering wheels on their backs. But crucially, the steering wheels aren't identical, and not everyone is able to steer everyone else. Secular progressives deliberately steer compromised Christian leaders in a worldly direction using credibility and empathy (and sometimes, money). Those compromised leaders then take up the progressive cause (superficially baptized with Christian slogans) and steer soft-hearted Christians using empathy and a concern for their "witness." The compromised leaders and soft-hearted Christians overcome faithful resistance to the progressive drift using sticks and carrots, waving the banner of mission and evangelism and (subtly) threatening ostracism from respectable Christian circles. And frequently men who are otherwise faithful will go along with it all because "So-and-so is a good guy" and "I don't want to rock the boat." In this way, the progressive gaze comes to dominate, not because every Christian leader is consciously setting out to appease progressives directly, but because corporately, we've absorbed progressive categories, sensibilities, and hostilities by osmosis. The influence is indirect and atmospheric. As one friend put it, "A man drinking water downstream may have no idea that the river's source is polluted, but that doesn't prevent him from being poisoned by it."

Wolves and Hirelings

Jesus warned us about wolves in sheep's clothing, false prophets who masquerade as sheep in order to tear the church apart. Wolves don't always look like wolves. Often they present as sheep—weak, simple, and, at times, wounded and in need of care.

But hirelings are just as hard to recognize. A hireling looks like a shepherd, but prioritizes himself over the sheep: "He who is a hired hand and not a shepherd, who does not own the sheep, sees the wolf coming and leaves the sheep and flees, and the wolf snatches them and scatters them. He flees because he is a hired hand and cares nothing for the sheep" (John 10:12-13). The hireling uses the credibility of the shepherd, but has different priorities.

The term "hireling" gives the impression that such men are in it for the money, that they've been bought off with cold, hard cash. But the reality is that social approval is often the true currency. And frequently it's not approval from the world directly, but rather approval from the "right" kind of Christians—which, in recent years, has meant respectable, empathetic, and winsome (to the left). Such Christians are frequently difficult to resist because a) they are "nice guys," and b) they technically affirm the correct doctrines, which insulates them from criticism.

The progressive gaze explains the great variety of characters in these common scenarios: out-in-the-open wolves and worldly apostles, wolves in sheep's clothing and false prophets, real victims and inflated victims, sincere advocates and opportunistic cry-bullies, naive peacemakers and empathetic peace-mongers, confused sheep and refugees from the world, respectable hirelings and decent shepherds with hireling tendencies (or hireling moments), reactive shepherds who saw the issues while resisting foolishly, and sober-minded shepherds who were faithful at their post.

Where Do We Go From Here?

In light of all of this, what should we do? First, we ought to look at the cast of characters living beneath the progressive gaze and find ourselves. Have we compromised under pressure? Have our empathy and zeal led us astray? Have we avoided conflict to keep a false peace? Have we had hireling moments? Have we been steered? Have we steered others? The variety of possibilities allows for clarity and precision. We need not be woke ourselves in order to have been manipulated by the woke. And at this point, we ought to have enough honesty to admit that the winsome-to-woke pipeline is real.

In answering this question, it's good to be specific, especially if we're leaders. For example, consider the pastoral office. The apostle Peter calls elders to "shepherd the flock of God that is among you, exercising oversight" (1 Pet. 5:2). Shepherds care for the sheep. Shepherds lead the flock and feed the flock. Shepherds guide the flock to green pastures and still waters, and they guard and protect the flock from bears and wolves and roaring lions. They are attentive to the health and safety of their sheep. If the sheep begin to look sickly, shepherds examine their diet. If they come down with a disease, shepherds bring medicine to heal them. If a sheep falls down a crack in the earth, a shepherd pulls him out and sets him back on the path. If a lion attacks, a shepherd grabs his staff and uses it to defend his sheep, even at great cost to himself.

Shepherds do this by "exercising oversight." Oversight obviously includes sight. You can't exercise oversight if you can't see clearly and understand accurately. But oversight is more than merely sight. It's "sight + responsibility." To exercise oversight means that when you see a need, you are responsible to do something about it. You can't just see; you must also "see to it."

So then, if oversight is sight plus responsibility to act, this means that there are, broadly speaking, two main ways that leaders (and particularly, pastors) can fail.

First, they can fail to see clearly. They don't recognize when the disease is spreading in their flock. They don't see the pack of wolves creeping over the hill, or are deceived by wolves in sheepskins, or mistake real sheep for wolves. They don't see that the water was polluted. Failure to see, failure to discern, is a failure to shepherd well.

In the church context, elders might fail to see the false teaching that is spreading like gangrene among their sheep. In particular, deceptive teaching can enter into a community through any of its sub-ministries: men's ministry, women's ministry, children and youth ministry, counseling ministry. Elders might also fail to see destructive patterns of behavior that are beginning to take root among their people. This includes things like gossip and slander or ungodly suspicion, domineering leadership or passive leadership, blaming victims or weaponizing victims. Elders fail to exercise oversight if they fail to see when false beliefs and destructive patterns of behavior are spreading among their people.

Second, elders can fail to act. They see the disease, but they don't wisely apply the medicine. They see the wolves, but they cower in fear. They see the polluted water, but they don't move the flock to better pastures. Failure to act is also a failure to shepherd well the flock of God.

Again, in the church context, elders might fail to counter false teaching with the truth. Rather than patiently correcting error, they might coddle it and tolerate it. Or conversely, they might reactively escalate theological conflict without understanding the appeal of the error to their particular people. They might make mountains out of molehills (or molehills out of mountains), or botch the timing with impatience or sluggishness.

In confronting destructive patterns of behavior, elders might fail to speak with sober-minded clarity and sincere love. They might avoid confrontation out of the fear that some sheep will "vote with their feet" and find another church. They might give in to the impulse to say "Peace, peace," when there is no peace. In each of these situations, elders, even when they see the danger clearly, might lack the nerve to act wisely and intentionally to address the challenges before them. And in doing so, they fail to exercise oversight.

Once we identify our failures, whether failures of sight or failures of action, whether our discernment failed or our nerve failed, we ought to take responsibility for all of them, confessing them to God and, if appropriate, acknowledging them to others. No excuses, no blame-shifting, no exaggerations.

And finally, we must get out from under the progressive gaze. That censorious progressive sitting on your shoulder, critically evaluating everything you do? Knock him off and put Jesus in his place.

This means refusing to pare down the sharp edges of the truth in order to cater to progressive sensibilities (or any other sensibilities for that matter). Instead, assume the center. Believe that the Scriptures are both true and good for the world. Speak boldly, clearly, courageously, with no muttering and mincing of words. Refuse to be embarrassed by anything the Bible says. More than that, refuse to be embarrassed and steered by association with fellow Christians, even ones you disagree with. If God is unashamed to be called their God, why should you be ashamed to call them brothers?

Live beneath the gaze of God, in the sight of a happy Father who is pleased with you in Christ. Seek his approval above all else, and based on that approval, seek to love your neighbors and commend Christ with courage and compassion.

5

FEMINISM: QUEEN OF THE WOKE

IN THE LAST CHAPTER, I ARGUED THAT running beneath the ideological conflicts surrounding all things "woke" (race, sexuality, abuse, and LGBTQ+) is a common emotional dynamic involving untethered empathy—that is, a concern for the hurting and vulnerable that is unmoored from truth, goodness, and reality. In the modern context, empathy is frequently "a disguise for anxiety" and "a power tool in the hands of the sensitive."[1]

1. Friedman, *A Failure of Nerve*, 133.

Untethered empathy, in tandem with a desire for respectability and credibility under the progressive gaze, is the means by which various aggrieved groups have been able to steer communities into catering to greater and greater folly and injustice. And a key ingredient in making this steering effective is feminism. Indeed, we can't adequately address the dangers of empathy without considering feminism and its impact on the church.

Controversy in Carolina

As a launching point, let's consider a controversy involving Father Calvin Robinson, an Anglo-Catholic priest from the UK. On January 19, 2024, Fr. Robinson delivered a message at the Mere Anglicanism Conference in South Carolina on the topic "Critical Theory: Antithetical to the Gospel?" Rather than simply focusing on critical race theory or queer theory, Fr. Robinson went to the root of the matter and identified Marxism, liberalism, and feminism as the origin of the rest. In particular, he identified feminism as the gateway drug to critical theory in the church, calling women's ordination a "Trojan horse" and a "cancer."[2]

In doing so, Fr. Robinson was following in the footsteps of another Anglican intellectual, C.S. Lewis. In his famous essay "Priestesses in the Church?," Lewis notes that ordaining priestesses to Christian ministry seems to entail a number of other modifications to Christian theology,

2. Calvin Robinson, "Cancelled from Mere Anglicanism," *Calvin's Common Sense Crusade*, January 20, 2024, https://calvinrobinson.substack.com/p/cancelled-from-mere-anglicanism.

including addressing "Our Mother in Heaven," and the notion that Christ might just as well have taken a female form in the Incarnation. As Lewis notes, "Goddesses have, of course, been worshiped: many religions have had priestesses. But they are religions quite different in character from Christianity."[3] In his talk, Robinson ably described the ideological dimension of the slippery slope from feminism to other forms of critical theory.

More than that, he briefly described the social dynamics in play and connected them particularly to empathy.

> Generally speaking, men tend to be more theologically rigid, whereas women tend to be more theologically flexible. That is because men do not have the emotional intelligence of women. We are more black and white, meaning we tend to be logic-based when it comes to problem solving. Women tend to be more inclusive. They are more empathetic and tend to be more emotion-based when solving problems. You can see how that might be a problem when a group is claiming to be an oppressed minority, and the thing preventing them from attending Church is the cruel doctrines and the regressive scriptures we follow. Which empath wouldn't want to compromise in order to make a so-called oppressed minority feel included?

To expand on Robinson's point, he is correct that, in general, women are more empathetic than men. And, in itself, this is a God-given blessing. Empathy—that is,

3. Lewis, *God in the Dock*, 259.

vicariously experiencing the emotions of another—can be a wonderful thing in its place. It fosters connection and bonding. It's why women frequently act as the glue that holds communities together. Abigail Dodds describes some of the benefits of this God-given feature.

> Research shows that women in particular are more empathetic than men when seeing other people in pain. I think this reflects a wonderful design feature that God has given women that benefits not only any children we might have, but our entire communities.
>
> A woman who is sensitive to the feelings of others, especially their pain, will be a sort of first responder. She is able to move toward the hurting. She can sound the alarm that someone is in need. And very practically for mothers, she can sense her infant's need for food and sleep and attention. She can detect a downcast glance from her teenage daughter or son. She can tell if her husband is carrying some frustration from his workday. Doesn't this make sense with God's design for a woman? The one he called *helper* (Genesis 2:18)? What a gift God has given to women.[4]

Crucially, however, what is a blessing in one place is a curse in another. The same impulse that leads a woman to move toward the hurting with comfort and welcome becomes a major liability when it comes to guarding

4. Abigail Dodds, "The Beauty and Abuse of Empathy: How Virtue Becomes a Tyrant," Desiring God, April 14, 2020, https://www.desiringgod.org/articles/the-beauty-and-abuse-of-empathy.

the doctrine and worship of the church. As we've seen already, there are times—usually involving grave error or gross sin—when God forbids empathy and pity. If someone—even a close family member—enticed Israel to commit idolatry and abandon the Lord, God told them, "You shall not yield to him or listen to him, nor shall your eye pity him, nor shall you spare him" (Deut. 13:6–10). So also in the case of first-degree murder, or of bearing false witness in court (Deut. 7:16; 19:13; 19:21). In such cases, God was adamant that "your eye shall not pity them."

This principle is highly relevant for the church's leadership and governance (whether we're talking Anglican priests, Presbyterian elders, or Baptist pastors). Whatever other functions ministers may perform (administration, service, care for the sick), the *sine qua non* of the ministerial office is teaching and guarding the doctrine and worship of the church. In such situations, empathy and pity are a liability, not an asset.

To use a biblical example, when Moses came down the mountain in Exodus 32 and witnessed the gross idolatry of the Israelites, he said, "Who is on the Lord's side? Come to me." The sons of Levi gathered to him. He then told them to pick up their swords and to go to and fro through the camp, killing their brothers, companions, and neighbors. Their eye was not to pity those who had committed such evil. God's response to the Levitical obedience was to ordain them to the priesthood.

Similarly, in Numbers 25, when the Israelite man strutted through the camp with his idolatrous Midianite bride (which we ought to regard as the very first Pride parade), Moses and the elders of Israel wept at the tent of meeting. Phinehas, however, took action, following the man and woman into their tent and driving his spear through both of them (presumably while in coitus). And God responded by saying, "That man will make a great priest."

In other words, the Scriptures teach both by precept and example that God's ministers—those who serve in God's sanctuary—must be "jealous with his jealousy" (Num. 25:11). Our zeal for God's holiness must supersede our natural love for our family and friends and neighbors. The truth of God, the right worship of God, must be so precious to us that we will not compromise or buckle even in the face of natural affection or under the influence of pity and empathy. The relevant application for us, as Fr. Robinson noted, is that the empathetic sex is ill-suited to the ministerial office, and thus women's ordination is indeed a watershed issue.

What Robinson Revealed

But my interest in the story is not merely in what Fr. Robinson said, but in what happened afterward. For the fallout was almost a textbook demonstration of his point, as well as a demonstration of another feature of the emotional dynamics involved when feminism encroaches upon the church. While Fr. Robinson's message was apparently well-received by many in attendance, others were decidedly nonplussed. And this was perhaps not surprising, since there were Anglican priestesses and advocates for women's ordination in the audience.

Reading the various accounts of Robinson's removal from the subsequent speaker panel, it is not difficult to see what happened. Fr. Robinson's talk was offensive to the priestesses in attendance; according to some accounts, a number of women (and men) walked out. No doubt some concerned and angry emails and texts were sent to the conference organizers, urging them "to do something about it." And so they did, disinviting Robinson from the remainder of the conference.

Here we see an additional layer to the emotional dynamics. Put simply, it is this: men struggle to deal with the unhappiness and displeasure of women. Put another way, female distress activates male agitation. Male empathy for an unhappy woman is frequently a disguise for his own anxiety and angst. This is especially true of "good" men, men who have been taught to be "servant leaders." We're all familiar with the modern social media phenomenon of "the white knight." A man sees a woman in distress (that is, engaged in online debate with a man), and comes to her aid by attacking her opponent with a vehemence and zeal that he would not have if another man was engaged in the same sort of ideological conflict.

Of course, this phenomenon is again a perversion of a good impulse. Women are the weaker vessel, and the masculine impulse to protect them is noble and right. Men are taught from a young age, "Don't hit girls. Treat them differently than the boys." But this noble principle is also subject to gross manipulation, especially in the modern egalitarian world in which women frequently enter the proverbial boxing ring. As Lewis taught us, "Battles are ugly when women fight."[5] This is true, not merely of physical war, but also of ideological and theological battles.

In fact, we might state the challenge in this way. Faithful men know how to resist unfaithful men. Good shepherds are willing to fight wolves. But even faithful men struggle to resist unfaithful women. She-wolves, especially ones who present themselves as victims, give faithful men fits because of the unavoidable asymmetries in play. What's more, ungodly women are often willing to exploit these asymmetries in order to steer entire communities. And it's not just the she-wolves who cause trouble—it's also the compromised (female) sheep, the ones who Paul calls "weak women," captured by false teachers due to their emotional instability, immaturity, and sin (2 Tim. 3:6–7).

A key part of the challenge here is a failure to recognize the egalitarian lie in all of its forms, particularly the lie that men and women are interchangeable. Male groups operate according to male norms—they're oriented to things (or ideas), comfortable with hierarchy, and willing to debate, challenge, and provoke one another directly. Female groups operate according to female norms—they're oriented to people (or feelings), prone to indirect and subtle communication and sublimated conflict, and

5. C.S. Lewis, *The Lion, The Witch, and the Wardrobe* (London: HarperCollins Children's Books, 2005), 109.

averse to open disagreement and overt hierarchies while being comfortable with excluding those who violate their social norms. In an excellent 2016 article on our modern crisis of discourse, Alastair Roberts ably describes the difference.

> The combative form of male competition is overt and on the surface: men are rough with each other and engage in forms of ritual combat, often as a form of bonding. Women's competition, by contrast, is largely carried out by such means as pressure to conform under the threat of social ostracization, leveraging male power to their advantage, recruiting males to attack people they dislike or rally to their aid, forming friendships or relationships with people of power or influence, gossip, cattiness, sassiness, sabotaging other people's reputations, veiled antagonisms in friendships, etc.[6]

Making generalizations like these already violates a number of feminist and egalitarian dogmas. But the more important generalization for our purposes is to note that *mixed* groups will inevitably tend to adopt female norms. Again, Roberts describes the toxic combination of male white-knighting and female modes of conflict.

> It is important that we recognize how certain prevailing forms of feminism have exploited male (protection

6. Alastair Roberts, "A Crisis of Discourse—Part 2: A Problem of Gender," *Alastair's Adversaria*, November 17, 2016, https://alastairadversaria.com/2016/11/17/a-crisis-of-discourse-part-2-a-problem-of-gender/.

> and concern for women's opinion) and female codes of behaviour (care, equality, empathy, etc.) to establish a context of discourse that is resistant to the operations of challenging truth. Threatening claims can be dealt with by denying the speaker a platform, by appealing to third parties for assistance in removing them, by attacking reputations and poisoning the well, by demonizing or encouraging extreme suspicion of people outside of the group, by attacking a person's presumed tone, by characterizing all rhetorical actions as veiled and illegitimate power ploys, by getting patron parties to police the discourse so that threatening positions can't be voiced, by using the threat of social ostracization to get people to self-censor, etc. All of these are classic feminine modes of handling social conflict.[7]

The unsurprising result, often unexpressed in public but noted in private among men, is frustration at the unfairness of the asymmetry of the mixed group. Direct speech is out; indirect speech is in. Open debate is out; emotional reasoning is in. Ideas are out; empathy is in. What seems most compassionate and empathetic in the moment is prioritized over what is good and wise in the long run. Violate the new rules and expect to be policed by white knights and sidelined for being quarrelsome, divisive, and rocking the boat, as Fr. Robinson discovered.

7. Roberts, "A Crisis of Discourse—Part 2."

Societal Suicide by Empathy

Of course, such pathological empathy is not restricted to the church. Our entire society is currently being destroyed by it. Running beneath the various forms of critical theory, whether feminist, racial, or queer, is a culture of victimhood flowing from toxic female empathy. Again, Alastair Roberts connects the dots.

> The social virtues that are elevated in women's groups tend to be things like inclusion, supportiveness, empathy, care, and equality. Through his and his students' research on the subject of 'social justice warriors', Jordan Peterson has identified that it refers to a real phenomenon in the world, but also suggests that it is specifically related to a maternal instinct: 'the political landscape is being viewed through the lens of a hyper-concerned mother for her infant.'
>
> This instinct causes all sorts of problems when expressed in an academic or political context. It infantilizes perceived victim, minority, or vulnerable groups (women, persons of colour, LGBT persons, disabled persons, etc.), perceiving them as lacking in agency and desperately in need of care and protection. When persons from such groups enter into the realm of political or academic discourse, they must be protected at all costs. Unsurprisingly, this completely undermines the manly code that formerly held, whereby anyone entering onto the field of discourse did so at their own risk, as a combatant and thereby as a legitimate target for challenge and honourable attack. The manly code calls

us all to play to strength, whereas the maternal instinct calls us all radically to accommodate to weakness. . . .

Feminist politics takes a more typically feminine form, majoring on the use of social leverage for feminist ends. If you think about it, the typical feminist political victory takes the form of persuading some other agency to do something or intervene on their behalf. It is a politics of empowerment and empowerment almost invariably rests upon the existence of some more fundamental power that acts as one's patron and comes to your aid against other parties. . . .

A politics of empowerment and a culture of victimhood go hand in hand. Just as the kid that bursts into tears and runs to their mother at the slightest provocation can use parental sanctions to empower them against others, so the feminist elevation of the rhetoric and ideology of victimhood serves to increase their social leverage. . . . Exaggerated vulnerability can be exploited as a means to gain power. The term 'crybully' has been coined to describe such weaponized victimhood and vulnerability.

It also creates a context that radically stifles strong and independent agency. The more that we privilege dependency and reliance upon third parties to intervene, the more we will start to resemble infants and the more those parties will adopt a smothering hyper-maternalism. Unsurprisingly, in those places where feminist theories and practices are most influential—on college campuses—we encounter the most stifling and neurotically protective

> institutions of all. The feminist rhetoric of strength is almost invariably allied to a rhetoric of vulnerability and victimhood.[8]

Empathy feeds the competitive victimhood mentality that is rampant in our society. In an empathetic society, victimhood confers invulnerability. Victims (both real and imagined) must be affirmed and validated and must not be questioned, challenged, or made to feel uncomfortable in any way, lest they be re-traumatized. Moreover, they are absolved of all responsibility for their actions, and they can count on others to excuse all manner of behavior out of a misguided sense of compassion. Just think of the rationalizations offered after riots done in the name of oppressed groups. The endgame of this mentality was well-expressed by a spokesman for Hamas after their brutal attack on Israeli citizens on October 7, 2024: "We are the victims . . . therefore nobody should blame us for the things we do. . . . Everything we do is justified"[9] (including, it seems, the rape and butchery of civilians).

The same empathetic logic lies beneath the societal indulgence of criminality that particularly plagues progressive cities (always provided that the criminal is a member of some aggrieved group), as well as the empathetic paralysis

8. Roberts, "A Crisis of Discourse—Part 2."

9. "Hamas Official Ghazi Hamad: We Will Repeat the October 7 Attack, Time and Again, until Israel Is Annihilated; We Are Victims–Everything We Do Is Justified," *MEMRI TV*, October 24, 2023. https://www.memri.org/tv/hamas-official-ghazi-hamad-we-will-repeat-october-seven-until-israel-annihilated-victims-everything-we-do-justified.

that prevents Western nations from wisely and justly addressing the challenges of both legal and illegal immigration. Compassion for refugees and "kids in cages" is used to open the border to millions of able-bodied young men.

But nowhere is this pathological feminine empathy more evident than in the various controversies surrounding transgenderism. Louise Perry succinctly draws the connection.

> Mentally ill misfits inspire compassion in women, particularly childless women looking for an outlet for their maternal instincts. When women view trans people as hyper-vulnerable—and trans activists have worked very hard on promoting that view—there's no way that women will call a "trans woman" a man, even if it means letting Bruno into the girls' locker room.[10]

Nature abhors a vacuum. As Lewis once wrote about equality, "[W]here men are forbidden to honor a king they honor millionaires, athletes, or film-stars; even famous prostitutes or gangsters. For spiritual nature, like bodily nature, will be served; deny it food and it will gobble poison."[11]

The same is true for our familial nature. However much our society may seek to be free of the dependence and duties of the family, human nature remains stubborn. If a woman

10. Louise Perry, "Cancel Culture is Girl Culture Part 1: How Feminine Aggression Works," *Maiden Mother Matriarch*, April 4, 2024, https://www.louiseperry.co.uk/p/cancel-culture-is-girl-culture.

11. C.S. Lewis, *Present Concerns*, ed. Walter Hooper (New York: Harcourt, 1986), 20.

rejects a husband, her desire for provision and protection remains; she will simply seek it in Big Government or Big Business. Rather than build her own house under her husband's headship, she will build Target or Goldman Sachs. The same is true for the desire to nurture and raise children. If a woman refuses to marry and have kids, she will seek to nurture and care for others. And when it is untethered, feminine empathy will fixate on the most demented and deranged individuals and groups. We see the bizarre spectacle of the proverbial "Mama Bear," but instead of protecting her own children, she's advocating for mentally unstable men to be allowed to compete against girls. How did Frankenstein end up on the podium accepting the gold medal for women's swimming (and cycling, and track, and weightlifting)? How did Frankenstein become prom queen? How did Frankenstein end up in the girls' locker room, showering with your thirteen-year-old daughter? Because Medusa let him in.[12]

How to Fight

In the face of these challenges, both inside and outside the church, the solution in some circles is to fight feminine fire with feminine fire. If a female teacher is leading God's people

12. For an excellent application of the dangers of untethered empathy, directed to a female audience, see Allie Beth Stuckey, *Toxic Empathy: How Progressives Exploit Christian Compassion* (New York: Sentinel, 2024). Stuckey explores five common progressive political slogans through the lens of toxic empathy: "Abortion Is Health Care," "Trans Women Are Women," "Love Is Love," "No Human Is Illegal," and "Social Justice Is Justice."

astray, find a faithful female Bible teacher to answer her. If a deranged man wants to use the women's restroom, let a female politician lead the charge to "protect women's spaces."

But outsourcing the fight against she-wolves and demented men to conservative shepherdesses and female magistrates is itself a subtle form of capitulation. Faithful women in the church expect faithful men to guard and protect the flock. And many of the female politicians who are resisting the trans-insanity made a name for themselves by "breaking the glass ceiling," invading traditionally male spaces (such as the military), and upending natural marriage in favor of same-sex mirage. In other words, they simply want to turn the clock back to an earlier stage of feminist rebellion. On top of that, there will never be enough godly, faithful women to meet the challenge, since the vast majority of them are too busy being faithful at their posts—raising their children, managing their homes, and serving God and his people in all the ways that are fitting and proper.[13]

13. Some may wish to point out the irony of my criticisms, given my commendation of Allie Beth Stuckey's book and given that Rosaria Butterfield wrote the foreword to this book. But, of course, there is no inconsistency at all. The issue is not whether a godly woman is able to rebuke feminist error. She clearly is, and God bless her for it. The issue is when capitulating and cowardly men put forward godly women instead of rebuking and correcting the error themselves, such as when Barak insists that Deborah lead the army, and loses the glory of the victory as a result. Yes, battles are ugly when women fight, as Lewis wrote in *Narnia*. But Father Christmas still gave Susan her bow and Lucy her dagger. In other words, when your back's against the wall, it's fitting for Christian women to imitate the unnamed woman in Judges 9 and drop the millstone on the wicked king's head. Or be like Jael and drive a tent peg through the bad guy's temple. But neither example supports the notion that women should aspire to combat, whether physical or ideological.

So then, if fighting feminine fire with feminine fire is out, what then should we do?

First, we must be alert to the particular battle in our denomination or church. Among Anglicans in North America, women's ordination is clearly the issue, and the present compromise is unstable and unworkable in the long-term. In the Southern Baptist Convention, the ongoing fight over female pastors is a clear battle line. In the Presbyterian Church in America, the same feminist impulse lurks beneath the principle that "A woman can do anything an unordained man can do." In nondenominational churches, the form the issue often takes is the pressure to get more women "up front" (not to preach, but to make announcements, read Scripture, etc.) or to make sure that more women are "in the room where it happens." You know you have a problem when there's a repeated pattern of all-male elder meetings in which a difficult decision is made that draws clear lines, and then, after the elders have gone home and talked to their wives, the emails and texts start flying: "Brothers, I've been praying about it, and I think we need to reconsider our decision . . ."

In all of these cases, conservative churches and denominations are in the early stages of sliding down the slippery slope pioneered by the mainline, as described in detail by Wayne Grudem in *Evangelical Feminism: A New Path to Liberalism?*[14] As Fr. Robinson noted in his address, the

14. Wayne Grudem, *Evangelical Feminism: A New Path to Liberalism?* (Wheaton, IL: Crossway, 2006).

move to ordain women in the Anglican Church opened the floodgates of liberalism.

> Naturally speaking, women who are conservative or orthodox in their theology will not believe that women can become men, or that women can be priests, and therefore in general do not put themselves forward for training for Holy Orders. So, the kind of women going forward for ordination tended to be liberals by design. This meant that when the Church decided it needed a ratio of 1:1, an 'equality' of men and women, what actually happened was that the Church was flooded with liberals.[15]

To mix metaphors, that slippery slope is a one-way train with four stops. Stop 1: "I'm Not *That* Kind of Complementarian." Stop 2: "I'm Neither Complementarian Nor Egalitarian." Stop 3: "I'm Egalitarian." Stop 4: "Sodomy Is Cool." The frequent move from egalitarianism to the affirmation and celebration of homosexuality is not so much a slippery slope, but simply what cancer does when left untreated. So the first step in battling the cancer of feminism is to recognize *how* the cancer is expressing itself in your particular community.

Second, having recognized where the rot is, it's imperative to dig deep roots in God's revelation, both in Scripture and nature. For forty years, evangelicals have referred to the biblical teaching of male headship in the home and

15. Robinson, "Cancelled from Mere Anglicanism."

the church as complementarianism, since men and women have *complementary* roles in marriage, family, and religious life. But in recent decades, many have begun to recognize fault lines within the complementarian camp, distinguishing between broad and narrow complementarianism (or thick and thin complementarianism, or hard and soft complementarianism). Broad/thick/hard complementarians want to apply male and female differences to many more areas (in the church and in society), whereas narrow/thin/soft complementarians only apply male and female differences in a few specific areas. This distinction is helpful. But I think there's a more fundamental difference between these groups. Let me suggest that the key division in all of the denominations mentioned above (except the ACNA, which already has egalitarian churches within it) is between natural complementarianism (or patriarchy) and ideological complementarianism.

This fundamental difference has to do with the relationship between Scripture and nature. According to natural complementarians, the biblical restriction of the ministerial office to qualified men simply cuts with the grain of God's design in creation. As I've argued elsewhere, biblical imperatives are built on divine indicatives.[16] Nature and Scripture speak with one voice.[17] Male headship in

16. Joe Rigney, "Indicatives, Imperatives, and Applications: Reflections on Natural, Biblical, and Cultural Complementarianism," *Eikon*, May 23, 2022, https://cbmw.org/2022/05/23/indicatives-imperatives-and-applications-reflections-on-natural-biblical-and-cultural-complementarianism/.

17. Joe Rigney, "With One Voice," *Eikon*, June 5, 2019, https://cbmw.org/2019/06/05/with-one-voice/.

the home is unavoidable. It's not a command but a baseline reality; it's a fact, and the only question is whether a husband will be a faithful head or an unfaithful head. Likewise, male leadership in the church is simply an outworking of the way that God made the world and the way that he is remaking it in Christ. The Pauline restriction in 1 Timothy 2 is built on God's creational design, a design that is testified in Genesis 1–2 and manifested in the concrete ways that he has made men different from women. Thus, for natural complementarians, male leadership outside the home and the church is normal and expected. (Incidentally, this is why the Bible regards a nation ruled by women and children as a sign of God's judgment; see Isa. 3:12.)

Ideological complementarianism, on the other hand, regards the biblical commands about male leadership in the home and the church as an arbitrary law overlaid on a neutered nature. At root, men and women are interchangeable, but God has inexplicably assigned men to be the head of their homes (which means that they have the tie-breaking vote in extreme circumstances) and to be elders in the church (which means they serve the congregation by doing whatever they want). The biblical restrictions, insofar as they exist, are ideology imposed on nature, not fitting commands derived from nature and clarified and reinforced by Scripture. In other words, ideological complementarians are egalitarian at heart, and they maintain their complementarianism only because of a handful of verses in Paul's letters—and once they are able to rationalize and embrace the egalitarian contortions of those passages, they take the Feminist Train to Stop 3.[18]

Given this difference, the starting place for resistance must be an unashamed embrace of reality. As I'm fond of saying, the first imperative is to love the indicative. The first command is to love God and the way that he has made the world. In this case, that means gladly embracing, without embarrassment, the reality that men and women are wonderfully different and complementary, and that these differences are relevant in all areas of life. What's more, it means celebrating (again without shame or embarrassment) the biblical teaching that accounts for, clarifies, and

18. The distinction between natural and ideological complementarianism, I think, also explains how certain charismatic and Pentecostal churches have in large measure avoided the further spread of liberalism while allowing for female pastors. My suspicion is that these churches are naturally complementarian—they recognize and gladly embrace that God made men and women differently and with different callings and abilities, and they practice this in their homes and welcome it in society. The adoption of female pastors is not driven so much by feminism and its impulses, but rather by their charismatic theology that links the Spirit's ongoing prophetic ministry (which is extended to both men and women) to the pastoral office. In other words, the normal and natural order of complementarianism is, in effect, suspended by the supernatural work of the Spirit in particular contexts. In that sense, the Pentecostal view is almost the reverse of ideological complementarianism. Instead of an interchangeable egalitarianism with a few positive laws sprinkled over the top for inexplicable reasons, this is a supernatural charismatic positive law imposed on an otherwise patriarchal world. On top of this, charismatics tend to be more immune to popular, respectable ideologies (such as feminism and wokeness) because many charismatic churches are lower/working class, and because they are already socialized to embrace stigmatization for their charismatic practice. As one charismatic pastor put it, "If you're open to praying in tongues, you're not easily embarrassed."

further grounds the reality of what it means to be men and women. We are equally made in God's image, yes, but men are the head, and women are the glory. From this happy embrace of reality, we can then apply the steady pressure necessary to not only remove the feminist infection from our churches, but also to commend God's design for men and women to a rebellious and confused world.

Applying this sort of steady pressure in the church and in the world will require steady men, sober-minded leaders who possess a clarity of mind, a stability of soul, and a readiness to act. They must be clear-headed, humble, and willing to take the lumps that will inevitably come.

And so let me close with a word to normal pastors, church leaders, husbands, and fathers. I know that this isn't the fight that you want. You wish we lived in a day when the cultural battles centered on the doctrine of the Trinity or the historicity of Christ's resurrection or some other theological doctrine. And in a way they do. Beneath our battles over manhood, womanhood, the family, and sexuality is the fundamental question: Who is our God? Are our feelings and passions and desires our god? Or is Jesus, the crucified and risen Messiah, the Lord of Heaven and Earth? So plant your flag on the Lordship of Christ.

But the pressing issues in our day are anthropological—what does it mean to be human? And the fight is with Medusa and Frankenstein (and Lilith and the Harpies and Goliath and the Cyclops and any number of other monsters spawned from the Dragon who stands behind them all). You can't avoid it. And the enemies of God won't fight fair. If you successfully and effectively resist the cancer of feminism, you will be called an abuser or an abuse-enabler. They will do this because these are the labels that continue to have substantial social leverage ("racist" and "misogynist" are all tuckered out). Your words will be twisted, and they will attack you based on partial knowledge of situations they haven't a clue about. They will stir up a cloud of concern around your church or your ministry, in hopes that others will learn their lesson and stay in line. And for a variety of reasons, ranging from simple prudence to pastoral confidentiality, you won't be able or willing to correct them. Hearsay will be enough to hang you, and the strawmen they construct will all bear your face. They will insist that you can't fight feminism *and* protect the vulnerable.

But here's the thing: you can. Not only that, you must. Resist Medusa (and the toxic empathy she rode in on) *and* protect the weak from actual predators. While you must not uncritically accept every accusation as true, you must take every accusation seriously. When horrific things happen, as they will in a fallen world and a demented culture, you can, by the grace of God, act to decisively deal with it. Have compassion on victims. Call the cops. Purge the evil. Heal the wounded. Preach the gospel of free grace to all, and call them to a costly obedience.

In the meantime, teach your church and family how to cheerfully endure false accusations and slander. Rejoice when they utter falsehoods against you (while making sure the falsehoods are false). Teach your sons to honor women as the weaker vessel. Teach your daughters to resist the manipulations of flatterers, whether the men who try to bed them or the women who try to absolve them of all moral agency. Work the principles of biblical justice deep into your bones so that you don't get swept away by the passions of the mob. Trust Christ. Grow in sober-mindedness. Act like men. Be strong.

In short, develop the kind of Christian fortitude that will enable you to endure the hurt feelings of priestesses and lady pastors, as well as the agitation and pressure of the nice guys. Cultivate the moral strength and stamina to resist the inevitable emotional sabotage and manipulation while offering true care and compassion.[19] Who is sufficient for these things? By the grace of God, we can be.

> Therefore, my beloved brothers, be steadfast, immovable, always abounding in the work of the Lord, knowing that in the Lord your labor is not in vain. (1 Cor. 15:58)

19. For a fuller exposition of this sort of sober-minded leadership, see the companion volume: *Leadership and Emotional Sabotage: Resisting the Anxiety That Will Wreck Your Family, Destroy Your Church, and Ruin the World* (Moscow, ID: Canon Press, 2024).

6
IN PRAISE OF COMPASSION

THIS BOOK HAS FOCUSED ON THE corruptions and abuses of compassion and its degeneration into untethered empathy. That's why it's important, in this final chapter, to write in praise of compassion. When a good thing has been weaponized for so long, it's tempting to reject the good thing itself (as opposed to its corruption). In the face of untethered empathy, it's tempting to succumb to apathy and indifference, to stand aloof, detached, and unmoved by suffering. It's tempting to close our hearts to those in need.

But the Scriptures are clear: if we see a brother in need and close our hearts to him, offering platitudes about being "warm and filled" instead of compassionate action, then God's love does not abide in us. Love is more than mouthing words; it involves deeds and truth (1 John 3:16–18). Compassion is still a virtue, despite its abuse.

What's more, compassion is too important, too valuable, and too powerful to leave in the hands of the empathetic. We must not be like Luther's drunken peasants, falling off on the apathetic and aloof side of the horse because others have fallen off on the side of untruthful pity and untethered empathy.

There are horrific evils in the world—physical and sexual violence and abuse, molestation and predation, psychological and emotional manipulation, slander and malicious gossip and a thousand other ways that human beings are cruel and wicked to one another. Those who have endured great evil at the hands of the wicked ought to receive our sincere and heartfelt compassion, and such compassion ought to move us to seek their healing and restoration and to pursue justice on their behalf.

But it's precisely the horror of the great evils in the world that leads me to insist on the need for *tethered* compassion. Our sympathy, if it is to remain faithful, must be anchored to what is true and good. Otherwise, the passion of pity will blind us and lead us astray. In fact, perhaps the simplest way to express what I've been seeking to do with pity is to encourage us to treat it like we do the other passions—desire, fear, anger, grief, etc. With these normal human passions, we all recognize that there are faithful and unfaithful versions. Pure desire and impure desire. Holy fear and unholy fear. Righteous anger and unrighteous anger. Godly grief and ungodly grief. The same is true of pity. So perhaps we can modify and apply some Pauline statements.

"In your anger do not sin" (Eph. 4:26, NIV). In your pity, in your compassion, do not sin.

"The anger of man does not produce the righteousness of God" (James 1:20). Neither does the pity or empathy of man.

Passions are powerful and must be tethered to what is good and governed by what is true.

Sober-Minded and Compassionate

Insisting on tethering our pity means that we must labor to be both sober-minded and compassionate, in that order. In other words, sober-mindedness is a prerequisite for faithful compassion. Sober-mindedness includes a clarity of mind, a stability of soul, and a readiness to act. Our minds are clear—they are not clouded by raging passions. Our souls are stable—we are not tossed by storms of passions. And we are ready to act—with a clear vision and ballast in our boat, we are ready to act wisely and faithfully. To be sober-minded is to be mature, having our passions governed by what is true and good through the habitual exercise of trained emotions.

Compassion is one of those trained emotions. Sober-mindedness enables godly compassion. I've sat and wept with a family who lost their eleven-year-old boy in a farming accident. I've grieved with families who have lost mothers to brain cancer. I've counseled and shepherded victims of various kinds of abuse. When faced with suffering, we must weep with those who weep (Rom. 12:15). Tethered compassion is not tepid compassion. We must join them in their sorrow. In doing so, we should labor to communicate four truths.

First, "This is hard." This is an objective statement about the situation. It's an acknowledgement of the difficulty and depth of the pain.

Second, "I know you feel that way." We communicate that we see and recognize their emotions, acknowledging their felt reality.

Third, "I'm with you in this." This is gospel presence, and it includes some measure of emotion-sharing, but without necessarily endorsing or affirming all that they are experiencing. By sharing the emotions of the afflicted (including their negative and painful emotions), we seek to build connection, to build trust, to cross the divide that so often isolates the sufferer from everyone else.

Fourth, "I have hope." In other words, we are tethered to Christ, clinging to him for dear life. The ultimate goal of emotional connection is to bring the sufferer to Christ so that he can comfort and heal them. Emotion-sharing serves compassion, and compassion moves us to loving action, just as compassion so often moved Jesus to act to help the hurting in the gospels (Matt. 9:36; 14:14; 15:32).

"This is hard. I know you feel that way. I'm with you in this. And I have hope." This is sober-minded and faithful compassion, the kind that enables us to offer true comfort to the hurting.

The apostle Paul tells us that we are the channels for the comfort of God. The God of all comfort has chosen to comfort his people in their affliction through his saints (2 Cor. 1:3–7). We all share in Christ's sufferings; therefore, we all may share in God's comfort and extend that comfort to others in Christ.

A number of years ago, I caught a glimpse of one form that such comfort takes in Dostoyevsky's novel *The Brothers Karamazov*. In a brief interaction over three pages, God helped me to see more clearly how to bring wisdom and tethered compassion together to comfort the grieving.

The Elder and the Grieving Mother

Father Zosima is a Russian monk and the mentor of Alyosha Karamazov, the hero of the novel. Early on, we are introduced to Father Zosima as he shepherds and comforts a group of women who have come to him burdened with various griefs, trials, and tragedies. These women have come with an unquenchable grief, a grief that breaks forth from silence into tears and lamentation. These lamentations "ease the heart only by straining and exacerbating it more and more. Such grief does not even want consolation; it is nourished by the sense of its unquenchableness.

Lamentations are simply the need to constantly irritate the wound."[1]

One such woman is a grieving mother who has buried her four children. The death of her last son at two years old has completely wrecked her. Her soul is wasted over him. Everything in her home reminds her of her little boy and sends her spiraling into despair.

In her grief, she has left her home, abandoned her husband, and lost herself in sorrow. She has come to Zosima seeking she knows not what. But Zosima is ready to meet her in her grief with the kind of wisdom and compassion that we need to comfort those in similar afflictions.

Weep, but Rejoice

So, what does Zosima do? First, he tells her a story of another grieving mother who was comforted by a great saint. In the story, the saint encourages the grieving mother by reminding her that infants who die are presently rejoicing with the angels in God's glorious presence.

Now, such a story creates space in the heart of the grieving mother. To listen to the story, she must step outside her grief and consider what was said to the other mother. And of course, Zosima tells her the story so that she can come to see herself in it. He echoes the counsel of the saint in the story, though with a twist. Whereas the saint says,

1. Fyodor Dostoyevsky, *The Brothers Karamazov*, trans. Constance Garnett (Simon & Brown, 2018), 54.

"Rejoice, and do not weep," Zosima says, "Weep, then, but also rejoice."[2]

So then, Zosima first takes the grieving mother out of herself and into a story, hoping that she might find herself and learn to weep, but also to rejoice.

The grieving mother brings the lesson home; Zosima's words echo what her husband Nikitushka had told her. He, too, had sought to encourage her with the presence of their son before God's throne. But grief overpowers this truth. Wherever her child is, he's not here with her. The reality of her son's absence emotionally overpowers the truth of her son's presence with God. All she can think of is his little voice saying, "Mama, where are you?" and his little feet pattering across the floor, and his laughter and shouting and joy. And now he's gone, and she'll never hear or see him again.

Weep, but Remember

As the woman collapses into tears, Zosima speaks a second time, this time placing this grieving mother in a biblical story. "This is Rachel of old 'weeping for her children, and she would not be comforted, because they are not,'" he says (see Jer. 31:15). There is a godly refusal to be comforted in one's grief, as with Rachel. Zosima, in essence, grants permission for this woman's refusal to be comforted. "Do not be comforted," he says. "Do not be comforted, but weep." But then he adds, "Only each time

2. Dostoyevsky, *The Brothers Karamazov*, 55.

you weep, do not fail to remember." Remember where your son is . . . and with Whom.

And with these words, Zosima points the way forward. For now, refuse to be comforted. Like Rachel, lean into the sorrow. But as you press in, remember the goodness and kindness of God. And in time, weeping with remembrance will turn lamentation into "quiet joy," and bitter tears into "tears of quiet tenderness." Weeping may last for the night (and the night may last for a long time), but joy comes in the morning.

What Is His Name?

Zosima is not done. Having pointed the way forward, he himself leans into the suffering. He promises to remember her child and her in his prayers, and he asks for the child's name. She responds:

> "Alexei, dear father."
>
> "A lovely name! After Alexei, the man of God?"
>
> "Of God, dear father, of God. Alexei, the man of God."
>
> "A great saint! I'll remember, mother, I'll remember, and I'll remember your sorrow in my prayers."

A small interchange, but I think it is highly significant. In asking for the child's name, Zosima communicates that he truly sees this woman, in all of her grief and pain. And he offers to join her in it. While she labors to weep and remember the mercy of God, Zosima will labor to remember her sorrow and her son. What's more, he affirms her son's name, connecting it to a saint from the past. He dignifies this mother and her son and, in doing so, builds a further connection.

Weep, but Return

But Zosima has one final step, a call to action. Not only does he promise to remember little Alexei and his grieving mother, but he goes on to say, "I'll remember your husband too." This mother is not the only one who is grieving. Her husband has lost not only his son, but his wife as well. By bringing him to mind, Zosima sets the stage to exhort this grieving mother and put her back on the path of healing.

Zosima says, "It is a sin to desert him. Go to your husband and take care of him." This, too, is love and comfort. Zosima is reminding her, "Yes, you may weep. Yes, you may refuse to be comforted for a time (and even a long time). But in your weeping, do not sin. In your grief over this tragic loss, do not abandon God's calling on you in the present."

And Zosima's words have their effect. The grieving mother exclaims, "I will go, my dear, according to your word, I will go. You've touched my heart. Nikitushka, my Nikitushka, you are waiting for me!" And she sets out on her long pilgrimage home.

Stories That Point to The Story

Of course, this little vignette is simply a story in a novel. But as in this brief conversation, stories are powerful.

Stories are soul food, as one author puts it. And they can help us in soul care.

Stories can help us to gain perspective, to step outside of our own lives in order to reflect on reality. Stories can point us to The Story, so that we can find ourselves in God's narrative when we're lost and adrift. Stories can direct us to the truth, helping us to remember and to connect both with God and with one another. And stories can direct us to action—to remind us of God's call upon us—so that we might walk in the light as he is in the light.

The Compassion of Christ

I'll end this book where we began—with the compassion and love of Christ. "We do not have a high priest who is unable to sympathize with our weaknesses, but one who in every respect has been tempted as we are, yet without sin" (Heb. 4:15). He has been made like us in every respect so that, as a merciful and faithful high priest, he is qualified to make propitiation for our sins. More than that, "because he himself suffered when tempted, he is able to help those who are being tempted" (Heb. 2:18).

What does the compassion of Christ, the love of Christ, look like? When my son was younger, he had a little stuffed lamb. When you squeezed it, the lamb sang, "Jesus loves me, this I know, for the Bible tells me so."

Jesus loves me. Words simple enough for my son to understand. Jesus loves me. Words that, according to Paul, surpass all human knowledge (Eph. 3:19). So unfathomable is the love of Jesus that we need Spirit-wrought strength to comprehend its length and width and height and depth.

That's one reason the story of Lazarus in John 11 is so precious. In this story, we see both the simplicity of the love of Jesus and its incomprehensibility. "Jesus loved Martha and her sister and Lazarus" (John 11:5). He loved them. And he loves us. And this story shows us just how surprising and unfathomable that love can be.

When Jesus Is Confusing

To refresh the story, Lazarus is ill. His sisters send word to Jesus, and Jesus decisively declares, "This illness does not lead to death. It is for the glory of God" (John 11:4). This prepares us for something big. As readers, we're primed for a sign—for a public supernatural act that demonstrates who Jesus is, like turning water into wine, or feeding five thousand, or healing a crippled man, or making a blind man see.

But then confusion sets in. When the sisters send word to Jesus—"Lord, he whom you love is ill" (11:3)—they clearly expect him to come. And yet Jesus delays: "So, when he heard that Lazarus was ill, he stayed two days longer in the place where he was" (11:6). He waits two more days after getting the news. It's confusing.

When Jesus tells his disciples about Lazarus, he seems to speak in riddles: "Lazarus has fallen asleep, but I go to awaken him" (11:11). That's good, the disciples say: if he's asleep, he'll wake up. But then Jesus tells them, "No, Lazarus has died." Is Jesus talking about sleep or death? It's confusing.

All along, Jesus's emotional responses are puzzling as well. To his disciples, he says, "Lazarus has died, and for your sake I am glad that I was not there" (11:14–15). Really? Our friend has died, and you're glad? That's confusing. But when Jesus arrives, he is troubled and weeps (11:33–35). If he's glad, why is he weeping? If he's weeping, why did he say he was glad? It's confusing.

At the tomb, Jesus tells them to remove the stone (11:38–39). But Lazarus has been dead for four days. He is dead-dead. Soul-has-left-the-body-and-gone-to-Sheol dead. Body-is-decaying-in-the-tomb dead. Why remove the stone now? It's confusing.

And hanging over the entire story is one confusing thought. Both sisters give voice to it:

> Martha: "Lord, if you had been here, my brother would not have died" (11:21).
> Mary: "Lord, if you had been here, my brother would not have died" (11:32).

The repetition is telling, isn't it? What have Mary and Martha been talking about for the last four days? What have they been saying to each other over and over again in the face of this tragedy? "If only he had been here."

Finally the mourners explicitly raise the question that haunts this whole story: "Could not he who opened the eyes of the blind man also have kept this man from dying?" (11:37).

And so, while Jesus's words at the beginning of the story prepare us for something big—for signs that display the glory of Jesus—the people in the story are living in confusion. This whole episode doesn't make sense. And the confusion matters because it's where most of us live.

Where We Live

Every one of us faces hardships, trials, suffering, affliction. And for Christians who believe that Jesus is all-powerful, all-wise, and all-good, the worst part is often this confusion. Whether it's illness (cancer, stroke, unexplained sickness, chronic pain); whether it's the death of someone we love (parent, child, sibling, friend); whether it's persecution, opposition, or enmity; whether it's anxiety, doubt, depression—here's what we know:

1. Jesus is able to fix this. He's omnipotent. We know he could fix anything, if he so chose.
2. In his compassion, Jesus has fixed these sorts of things for others. He did heal the blind man. He did heal the official's son. That's what Mary and Martha want. And that's what we want too.
3. Jesus loves me.
4. And yet, the illness is still here, the death still happened, the persecution has intensified, and the darkness has not lifted.

We're constantly saying, "Couldn't you have prevented this, Jesus?" Like the sisters, we repeat over and over, "If only you had been here . . ."

This is where we live. In the dark, in the confusion, in the frustrated hopes and unfulfilled desires, in the riddles and the questions and the doubts. We live in the long days between our message to Jesus—"The one whom you love is ill"—and his confusing arrival later on. And that's where Martha and Mary lived. And yet, John insists from the beginning, "Jesus loved Martha and her sister and Lazarus" (11:5). So where is the love of Jesus in this story? We see the love of Jesus in six key words.

The Love of Jesus Waits

The first word is "so" (11:6). It's the most shocking word in the whole story. Jesus loved Martha and Mary and Lazarus. *So*, when he heard about the illness, he stayed two days longer. He loved them; *therefore*, he stayed. The love of Jesus kept him from going to heal Lazarus and sparing them the longest week of their lives.

Some Bible translators can't handle that word. They say, "Jesus loved them, and yet, when he heard, he stayed two days longer." In other words, despite the fact that he loved them, he waited. But that's not what John wrote. John said that Jesus loved them; therefore he waited. He loved them; therefore he let Lazarus die. He let Mary and Martha sit in their grief, their tears, their confusion, their questions.

"If Jesus would have been here. . . . Why wasn't he here? Why didn't he come right away?"

Because he loves you, Martha. Because he loves you, Mary. Because he loves you, Lazarus. The word "so" teaches us that the love of Jesus waits.

The Love of Jesus Weeps

The next two words are "Jesus wept" (11:35). This, too, is love. The crowds recognize it immediately. When Jesus weeps at the tomb of Lazarus, they say, "See how he loved him!" (11:36). And in this, we see the amazingly complex and righteous emotional life of our Lord.

On the one hand, he tells the disciples, "Lazarus has died, and for your sake I am glad that I was not there" (11:14–15). He's glad that he waited—because he loves them. And then, when he gets there, he weeps—because he loves them. More than that, he is deeply moved; literally, he's angry and indignant (11:33). Jesus sees Mary and Martha weeping, and he is indignant at sin and death and the way that it ravages those he loves.

This is so important to remember. Yes, the love of Jesus waits. It even rejoices in waiting. But he still meets us in our sorrow. When we come to him with our confusion and our questions—"Where were you? Why didn't you do something?"—he doesn't rebuke us. He says, "I know. Grief is great. I'm with you and for you. Bring your confusion. Yes, I waited. And I'm still with you because I love you."

The Love of Jesus Raises the Dead

Finally, three more words: "Lazarus, come out" (11:43). This, too, is love; it's the love of Jesus that raises the dead. Jesus doesn't just wait, and he doesn't just weep. He acts. He performs a sign that reveals the glory of God so that the Son of God may be glorified in it. After he waits, and after he weeps, he tells them to roll away the stone, and he prays out loud so that everyone knows what is happening (11:41–42). And then he looks at the tomb and calls out, "Lazarus, come forth!"

And Lazarus comes forth. The church fathers noted how important it was that Jesus said the name Lazarus. Had he not—had he simply said, "Come forth"—they speculated that all the tombs would have emptied, and the general resurrection would have happened right then and there. That's how powerful he is! But instead, Jesus calls forth one man, by name, and that man comes forth, hobbling out of the tomb, wrapped in graveclothes. And in the face of everyone's astonishment, Jesus says, "Unbind him, and let him go" (11:44).

Do You Believe This?

This deep, radical, often counterintuitive love is what the whole confusing story has been about. The waiting, the riddles, the confusion, the weeping, the raising: the whole story is designed to take us deeper so that we know the love of Christ that surpasses knowledge—not just that he cares for us, not just that he can do all things, not even just that he can raise the dead, but that he is the resurrection and the life.

> I am the resurrection and the life. Whoever believes in me, though he die, yet shall he live, and everyone who lives and believes in me shall never die. Do you believe this? (John 11:25–26)

This is where Jesus has been taking Martha. "Do you believe this? Even though your brother is lying in a tomb, even though you know that I could have prevented it—Martha, do you believe this?"

And so Jesus stands before us today. And as we sit with Martha in our confusion, because he loves us, he says to us, "Do you believe this?" When the cancer is still there. When the illness is still unexplained. When the headaches won't stop. When the pain is still oppressive. When the opposition won't let up. When the darkness hasn't lifted. When the doubts still weigh us down. When the body is still in the grave. When Jesus is not yet here. At that moment, before he raises the dead, he says to us, "Do you believe this?"

Jesus loved Martha and Mary and Lazarus. And he loves you. And because he loves you, he may wait. He may take you through unimaginable suffering and loss and pain. And when he does—because he loves you—he will still be with you. And someday, because he loves you, he will raise the dead. He will right every wrong and wipe away every tear.

And in the meantime, because he loves you, he is taking you deeper into his love. He is revealing his glory to you in the waiting and the weeping.

Jesus loves me, this I know, for the Bible tells me so.

Do you believe this?

Appendix A

ON PROVOCATIVE RHETORIC:

"The Sin of Empathy"

THE MOST COMMON CRITICISMS leveled against what I've written have been in relation to two issues. On the one hand, I'm accused of illegitimately redefining terms. On the other hand, I'm accused of overheated and misleading rhetoric. The latter criticism has even been leveled by those who share my substantive concern about untethered empathy but believe that the language of "the sin of empathy" is unhelpful and confusing.

I've addressed the issue of definitions in the opening chapter, so I'll simply summarize it here. The reality is that empathy is a contested term with a great variety of definitions. I know this because I have had numerous critics insist on various "true" definitions of empathy. I'm told that empathy is less than sympathy and compassion and in fact serves sympathy and compassion. I'm told that empathy is simply a synonym for compassion and sympathy. I'm told that sympathy and empathy are very different, and indeed empathy is the more loving response.

I'm told that empathy is emotion-sharing or perspective-taking or both. It's walking a mile in another's shoes. It's vicariously experiencing the same emotions as another person. Or it's an imaginative projection of a subjective state. And this doesn't even take into account the different contexts in which the term might be used—from medical to psychological to popular—and the ways that such contexts blur and change over time. As the opening chapter demonstrated, there is no single, standard definition of empathy.

My way of dealing with the definitional challenge has simply been to define very carefully what I mean and to avoid wrangling about words by being willing to translate the key concepts into different terms when necessary. Additionally, I want to stress once more that I'm not mainly concerned with the "true" definition of empathy, but with its use. The problem I'm addressing is not primarily philosophical or etymological, but functional and practical. Empathy, pity, sympathy, compassion—whatever terms you want to use, the key is to address the corruptions and distortions in the emotional dynamics.

The Rhetorical Challenge

But this leads to the rhetorical criticism—namely, that I provocatively use the phrase "the sin of empathy." It's the "the sin of ______" phrase that people struggle with. How might we address this criticism?

To begin, numbering empathy among the other passions may be clarifying. An article on "the sin of anger" or "the sin of sexual desire" or even "the sin of loyalty" is comprehensible to many, even though we all know that not all anger or sexual desire or loyalty is sinful (the same would be true for fear, anxiety, and grief). In each case, we naturally understand the phrase "sin of anger" to mean "sinful anger," and we would need to actually read the article to determine whether there were clear definitions and proper distinctions made.

The issue with "the sin of empathy" is that few people in the modern world can imagine empathy being sinful or negative. It is an incorruptible virtue, and thus, as Friedman noted, questioning its value is considered irreverent, if not sacrilegious. But it's precisely empathy's inviolable status that makes it such a powerful mask for corruption.

At this point, it's worth quoting Lewis again on the danger of separating mercy from justice.

> Mercy, detached from Justice, grows unmerciful. That is the important paradox. As there are plants which will

> flourish only in mountain soil, so it appears that Mercy will flower only when it grows in the crannies of the rock of Justice: transplanted to the marshlands of mere Humanitarianism, it becomes a man-eating weed, all the more dangerous because it is still called by the same name as the mountain variety.[1]

Notice the final phrase: the untethered and corrupt version is *more dangerous* because it is still called by the same name as the virtue. This is as true of empathy as it is of mercy. Empathy might refer to simple emotion-sharing. Well and good. Or empathy might refer to total immersion in the feelings of another, the power tool in the hands of the sensitive. The common term is what creates the confusion.

The question is this: is it legitimate to expose a real sin by using its assumed (good) name? Or must we always and only use distinctive and negative terms for the distortion (terms like "enmeshment" and "codependence")?[2]

My answer is simple: because vices typically hide within virtues, it is legitimate to attack the vice under its assumed name. Such a rhetorical approach is frequently used to

1. C.S. Lewis, *God in the Dock*, ed. Walter Hooper (New York: HarperOne, 1994), 326–327.

2. It is not lost on me that my critics frequently use terms drawn from modern psychology—and not merely descriptive terms like "enmeshment," "codependence," and "narcissism," but even evaluative terms like "toxic" and "unhealthy." While I see some value in the therapeutic framework and its vocabulary, my use of the word "sin" combined with a therapeutic term like "empathy" was undoubtedly jarring to many ears. Indeed, I've wondered whether a chief part of the confusion is the difficulty in bringing the therapeutic framework into conversation with a more classical moral framework.

arrest attention, and we are more than capable of recognizing when it's being employed. Here are a few examples, drawn from other book titles: *The Intolerance of Tolerance*, by D.A. Carson; *When Helping Hurts*, by Brian Fikkert and Steve Corbett; and *Toxic Charity*, by Robert Lupton.

In each of these cases, we recognize the rhetorical strategy in play. We know that Carson is not condemning all forms of tolerance. Not every attempt to help hurts, and not all charity is toxic. Instead, in each case, we mentally add quotation marks around the key terms: "tolerance," "helping," and "charity." The "sin of empathy" is clearly in this vein.

Lewis himself uses this rhetorical move when he unmasks the sins that frequently hide beneath the term Unselfishness. In *The Screwtape Letters*, Screwtape notes the success of the demonic philological arm in substituting unselfishness for the Christian virtue of Charity (much as folks like Brené Brown substitute empathy as an improvement on sympathy). Unselfishness is a negative term that emphasizes what *we're* giving up. Charity is a positive term that emphasizes the good we're doing for others. The value of the shift is that the demons can "teach a man to surrender benefits not that others may be happy in having them but that he may be unselfish in forgoing them."[3]

He goes on to note the ways that Unselfishness can mask very complicated forms of self-righteousness. One member of a family says they'd like to go out to eat. Another member says, "I'd prefer to stay in, but I'm willing to go out"

3. C.S. Lewis, *The Screwtape Letters* (New York: HarperOne, 2015), 141.

(in the spirit of Unselfishness). The first person withdraws the proposal in the same spirit of Unselfishness, not wanting to allow others to practice petty altruisms on him. Instead, he says, "I'm willing to do what everyone else wants." Immediately the whole family, all caught in the grip of Unselfishness, insists that they're each willing to do what everyone else wants as well. They seek to outdo one another in showing Unselfishness, with the result that "passions are aroused . . . and a real quarrel ensues with bitter resentment on both sides."[4]

Now at this point, someone might object, "But Lewis, these people aren't actually being unselfish; they're being the opposite. Their behavior is profoundly selfish and self-righteous. No one would define Unselfishness in the way that you have." And Lewis would no doubt reply, "Quite so. People rarely advertise their sins as such. Envy hides behind a mask of 'equality and justice,' greed behind a facade of 'blessing and prosperity,' laziness behind the desire to respect other people's space, busybody-ness behind the call to love and sacrifice for others, pride and superiority behind gratitude ('I thank you, God, that I'm not like that man . . .')." The Devil loves to hide real sins inside innocent phrases, and especially inside virtues. And like Lewis on the shift from Charity to Unselfishness, I believe that the shift from Compassion to Empathy is "of more than philological significance."[5]

4. Lewis, *The Screwtape Letters*, 141.

5. C.S. Lewis, "The Weight of Glory," in *The Weight of Glory and Other Addresses* (San Francisco: Harper, 2009), 25.

As a result, it has seemed good and right to me to use provocative rhetoric to make this shift clear. After all, provocation is not always wrong. Provoking thought is good. Arresting attention is good. Jesus, Paul, and the prophets were provocative. They made statements that were subject to misunderstanding and confusion.

More than that, provoking a reaction in one person is sometimes necessary to provoke thought in another. That's certainly been my experience in repeatedly addressing the sin of empathy. A number of readers have told me that they were initially skeptical of my arguments. But then they witnessed the overwrought reactions and misrepresentations of critics, and all of a sudden, the destructive dynamics became clear. The attempts at sabotage were obvious.

Of course, the use of provocative rhetoric demands a willingness to patiently correct confusion and endure misrepresentation from bad faith critics who simply want to sabotage and steer. As Paul says, "the Lord's servant must not be quarrelsome but kind to everyone, able to teach, patiently enduring evil, correcting his opponents with gentleness. God may perhaps grant them repentance leading to a knowledge of the truth, and they may come to their senses and escape from the snare of the devil, after being captured by him to do his will" (2 Tim. 2:24–26). While my efforts in this regard have no doubt been imperfect, after writing 30,000 words on the subject, no one can deny that I tried.

Appendix B

CORRUPT COMPASSION:

Recognizing a Devilish Strategy[1]

Letter 1

My dear Mugwort,

Your last letter reminds me of just how far you have to go in the science of tempting. Your whimpering and

1. This appendix was originally published as two articles for Desiring God: Joe Rigney, "Killing Them Softly: Compassion That Warms Satan's Heart," Desiring God, May 24, 2019, https://www.desiringgod.org/articles/killing-them-softly; and "The Enticing Sin of Empathy: How Satan Corrupts through Compassion," Desiring God, May 31, 2019, https://www.desiringgod.org/articles/the-enticing-sin-of-empathy.

excuse-making at your patient's growth in the virtue of compassion is unusually pathetic, even for you.

Of course, it is a setback, and, of course, you'll be reprimanded for it. But as a member of my department, I expect you to respond to these new challenges with the same courage and resilience that I would in your situation. Not that I would ever be in your situation; as I told you in previous letters, you must be wary of any growth in sympathy in your patient and make efforts to divert him into more fruitful pursuits. But the young never regard the wisdom of their elders, and now you are paying for your negligence.

Even as you suffer the necessary consequences, however, do not lose your head. Compassion, like all of the Enemy's qualities, is corruptible. In fact, the sheer intensity of its goodness means that, when corrupted, it becomes a most potent demon.

It is a strong feeling and retains its strength even after it has been diverted from the Enemy's service. This in fact is one of Hell's greatest triumphs: that we are able to steal the power and might of the Enemy's works and turn them to better uses. Even if we are unable to injure him with his vile weapons, we may at least injure his pathetic little statues on earth.

Your elders labor to hide whole systems of thievery in robes of compassion. As a lesser tempter, however, you must be content to corrupt compassion at the level of your individual patient. The simplest way to do so is to link compassion to another virtue, such as truth-telling, and then have the second virtue swallow it up. The Enemy wants the humans to have "bowels of mercy"; he wants them to practically ooze with sympathy and pity, which, though guided by reason, are nonetheless animated by deep feeling and affection.

You must instead quench the flame of feeling and substitute right thinking in its place. Teach him to regard "speaking the truth in love" as a redundancy, as though any true thing he said is loving whether or not it is fitted to the occasion, and whether or not he is the proper messenger for it.

I had a patient once who lived by the mantra "The most loving thing we can do for people is to tell them the truth" and was thereby constantly immunizing others against the Enemy's warnings and promises. His demeanor was so off-putting that words that might have been a great comfort to others in his family and his church (and therefore a great threat to us) became a byword and a mockery.

This tactic is especially useful for statements like "God works all things together for good." We, of course, deny the truth of this; it's only blind luck that some of our greatest assaults have been foiled as if by some deeper plan. Our efforts to wipe out the Enemy's chosen family a few millennia ago prove this all too well.

I remember when Scabface made his audacious proposal in the Infernal Council (I was a young tempter then, an aide to one of Scabface's rivals). His team would stoke jealousy among the twelve brothers, provoking them to kill the patriarch's favorite, using dreams that the Enemy sent the favorite as a pretext (another example of Hell corrupting the Enemy's works). Meanwhile, while the holy family was thus in turmoil, Slubgob's team would initiate a famine that would wreak havoc in the ancient world, with the aim of causing the entire company to starve. We had it all planned out. Send plenty and abundance first in order to lull the idiots into a false sense of security. Humans are notorious for thinking that the present state of affairs is permanent, when all of their histories demonstrate that such a belief is absolutely ludicrous. Then, when they think the good times will never end, break all supply of bread and watch them wither away and perish.

It was simply unlucky that the favorite rose to prominence in the way he did; we threw everything we had at him: discouragement, sexual temptation, slander and false accusation, being forgotten by those whom he helped and who owed him their lives and livelihoods. But he was constantly surrounded by that piercing fog of brilliance that indicates the Enemy's presence. Even then, we were not worried. Plans for the famine were proceeding apace. Who could have predicted that the favorite would rise so high in the pagan court? We had the Egyptian king and his whole household well in hand.

And how could we have foreseen that he would have the wisdom and wherewithal to prepare for the famine and save not only the Egyptians but his own ungrateful family? That he would have his own persecutors in his power, and simply forgive them, was so outlandish that none of Hell's prognosticators could ever have predicted it. Luck, Mugwort, dumb luck was our downfall.

But the worst of it is that the Enemy has made hay of such blind chance. He has the audacity to take credit for it! To claim that all things work together for good, that what we and the jealous brothers had intended for evil, he had always intended for good. The pretense to take credit for our work, as though we were merely his puppets. What propaganda! What froth and nonsense! Nevertheless, this "truth" has been great comfort to numerous of the Enemy's pawns, even as we have ripped everything from them, and were it actually true, it would no doubt demoralize even our fiercest tempters.

We can neutralize even this advantage of the Enemy. Render the claim "All things work together for good" into a platitude, into a trite saying that is most at home on greeting cards and kitsch. Let it flow easily from the lips of those who live in comfort and ease so that, rather than being a salve to the wounds of the afflicted, it further inflames their pain. The balm of Gilead becomes a source of resentment and bitterness.

Once you've trivialized the saying, you may use it to corrupt compassion. Use your patient's belief in it as a tool that he wields against the suffering. When he comes face to face with real affliction, make him think that the first and most important act of compassion is to correct the thinking of the sufferer.

When a woman is weeping over the loss of her child, questioning the Enemy's goodness, let him intrude with "All things work together for good." And teach him to say it in such a tone of voice that communicates the obviousness of its truth. Let him offer it as a correction thinly veiled as a comfort. That way, when the platitude is resisted, you can nurse in him the self-pitying feeling that "I was only trying to help."

Let him, however unintentionally, heap guilt and shame upon the grieving. Let him give the impression that the proper way to suffer is the Stoic way—unfeeling and confident in the face of loss. Build up the impression in his own mind; let him even practice it for himself and then turn his mode of suffering into a standard by which he evaluates others. In this way, you can even use his success in enduring affliction as a weapon against others.

Never let him suspect that his eagerness to insist upon this "truth" is actually owing to his (very reasonable) doubts about its truthfulness. His discomfort in the face of real suffering and sorrow leads him to turn the Enemy's potent weapons into platitudes that not only fail to comfort the afflicted but actually further afflict them.

You must bring him to a place where he attempts to steer the emotional vehicle of every sufferer that he comes across. Make him think that real displays of lamentation are an assault on the Enemy's character, and as a partisan of the Enemy, he must take up the cause and justify the ways of God to men, even to a grief-stricken mother.

Teach him to always look for the silver lining in other people's troubles. (Of course, make sure that he never looks for it in his own. Hell forbid that he ever actually learn to give thanks in all circumstances, including the ones that he finds most discouraging, frustrating, and sorrowful).

Make him into the sort of false comforter who always begins with "At least." "You've lost your job, but at least you have your health." "Yes, your child may be disabled, but at least he's alive." "Yes, you may be walking through barrenness, but at least you're married."

The trick is for your patient to try to cultivate gratitude in others by comparing their sufferings to greater ones. The mindset we want to see is the one that starts from the premise "It could always be worse," and then moves from that true but irrelevant statement to "And therefore you've no right to grieve as you are." As I've told you a thousand times, Mugwort, comparison is always a tempter's friend.

You may think that such errors would be easily avoided by the patient, but you'd be wrong. In the same way that they love to collapse virtues into each other (like they do with "speaking the truth" and "loving"), they equally love to abstract virtues from each other. Thus, it's no trouble to teach him to "be compassionate" (that is, "Speak truth with no regard for timing or propriety") while ignoring the Enemy's demand for patience, long-suffering, wisdom, and fitness.

In fact, this is one of the more amusing ways to fuddle the humans: At the exact moment that he is urging patience and joy to the grieving mother, he himself is being impatient about the fact of her ongoing sorrow. He finds her continued grief unendurable at precisely the moment when he is exhorting her to endure. The frustration resulting between two people on such occasions, especially if they are closely related, is one of the simple joys of a tempter's life.

But there are other and more delicious ways to corrupt compassion. Next week I'll teach you how to turn the virtue of compassion into the sin of empathy.

Your affectionate uncle,
Scratchpot

Letter 2

Really, Mugwort, I would have thought that a young and ambitious tempter would pay attention to the annual updates posted by the Infernal Philological Society. The fact that you had never heard the idea that empathy was a sin is enough to turn me into a centipede.

Your confusion in this case, however, is somewhat understandable. I've always said you were a gullible devil. It seems the Department of Propaganda has been too successful. Even our tempters have been taken in. As a result, it falls to me to explain again some of the elementary doctrines of our Father Below.

When humans are suffering, they tend to make two demands that are impossible to fulfill simultaneously. On the one hand, they want people to notice the depth of their pain and sorrow—how deep they are in the pit, how unique and tragic their circumstances. At the same time, they don't want to be made to feel that they really need the assistance of others. In one breath, they say, "Help me! Can't you see I'm suffering?" and in the next they say, "How dare you act as though I needed you and your help?" The sufferer doesn't want to be alone and demands not to be pitied. This makes their emotional turmoil in suffering not only delicious to our taste, but also highly combustible and unpredictable.

Now, sufferers have been placing such impossible demands on others from time immemorial. In response, our armies have fought for decades to twist the Enemy's virtue of compassion into its counterfeit—empathy. Since we introduced the term a century ago, we've steadily taught the humans to regard empathy as an improvement upon compassion or sympathy.

Compassion only suffers *with* another person; empathy suffers *in* them. It's a total immersion in the pain, sorrow, and loss of the afflicted. Under our influence, we've taught the humans to think, "Only a heartless and unfeeling beast could oppose such a total immersion, such a generous act of 'love.'" Our recent success in this conceptual migration has given us ample opportunity for mayhem.

Think of it this way: the Enemy's virtue of compassion attempts to suffer with the hurting while maintaining an allegiance to the Enemy. In fact, it suffers with the hurting precisely because of this allegiance. In doing so, the Christians are to follow the example of their pathetic and repulsive Master. Just as the Enemy joined the humans in their misery in that detestable act of incarnation, so also his followers are to join those who are hurting in their misery.

However, just as the Enemy became like them in every way but sin, so also his followers are not permitted to sin in their attempts to comfort the afflicted. Thus, his compassion always reserves the right not to blaspheme. It seeks the sufferer's good and subordinates itself to the Enemy's abominable standard of Truth.

Our alternative, empathy, shifts the focus from the sufferer's good to the sufferer's feelings, making them the measure of whether a person is truly "loved." We teach the humans that unless they subordinate their feelings entirely to the misery, pain, sorrow, and even sin and unbelief of the afflicted, they are not loving them.

This begins, of course, with the sufferers themselves. Our policy has been to teach sufferers to resent all resistance to their feelings. Any holding back, any perceived emotional distance—especially a distance that is driven by a desire to discover what would actually be good for them—must be regarded as a direct assault on their dignity and an affront to the depth of their suffering. As I said before, this is not difficult. A human in pain is practically primed to say, "You don't love me if . . ." and then to place entirely unreasonable demands on others.

Our task is to give this impulse a little push. We want their unreasonable demands to become ungodly demands. Not only must comforters refuse to actually offer words of comfort (which even their sniveling shepherds suggest is sometimes a prudent policy in the immediate aftermath of some calamity), but we want sufferers to subtly but forcefully demand that their comforters not even feel hope or joy or faith themselves. Total immersion must be granted, or "You don't love me." Anyone who refuses to jump through the hoops isn't being empathetic.

But our efforts don't end with the sufferer. We must also work on the comforter, the one who feels and acts with compassion. Picture the sufferer as someone being slowly overcome by quicksand. The compassionate person, desiring to help and comfort them, knows that he must enter into the pit with them.

However, he also knows that he'll only be able to help if he's tethered to something strong and sturdy outside of the quicksand. And so he enters the pit with one foot, while keeping the other on the solid ground. He reaches for the hurting with one hand, while holding onto a firmly rooted tree with the other. This is where your patient is now, looking at the various instances of suffering and affliction around him and desiring to help, comfort, and encourage those in the pit.

Your task is to compel him to jump in with both feet. As I've said, the sufferer will naturally be demanding it. You must increase the pressure by fostering in him a sensitivity to accusations of heartlessness. This is where our philological efforts have made your job much easier than you deserve.

By elevating empathy over compassion as the superior virtue, there is now an entire culture devoted to the total immersion of empathy. Books, articles, and social media all trumpet the importance of checking one's own beliefs, values, judgments, and reason at the door of empathy.

To refuse to fully endorse the feelings of the hurting, however blasphemous and false, is to re-victimize them. Maintaining the emotional independence necessary to rationally consider someone's good is "unhelpful," "heartless," "contrary to the spirit of Jesus." These terms can be used to browbeat your man into submission so that he never pauses to consider the true and lasting good of the one in pain, or the truthfulness and accuracy of their felt reality.

Once untethered from the truth, you'll find that your man is eminently steerable. Things that he would have regarded as foolish, sinful, and ungodly under normal circumstances will sail right along under the banner of empathy. Rightly used, empathy is a power tool in the hands of the weak and hurting. By it, we can so weaponize victims that they (and those who hide behind them) are indulged at every turn, without regard for whether such indulgence is wise or prudent or good for them.

When you can move your man from the bland but true belief that "feelings are important" to the false but potent impression that "feelings are all that's important," then you know that you have him. Properly conditioned and trained in this way, you will be able to steer him in any direction you choose.

As in many things, we must always keep in mind the Enemy's goals and ours. The Enemy aims to produce a fellowship of sufferings, with his accursed Son at the center of it. But fellowship requires fellows; that is, it requires distinctness. Fellows say, "We are together, and yet I am still I, and you are still you." This is a kind of union where one thing is united to another thing while still being itself.

In fact, if the Enemy is to be believed, creatures become more themselves when thus united. Of course, it is all lies, and in stoking empathy we are simply cutting with the grain of reality. Empathy goes beyond union to the more potent and dynamic truth of fusion, the melting together of persons so that one personality is lost in the other. Empathy demands, "Feel what I feel. In fact, lose yourself in my feelings."

In my last letter, I told you that compassion, when untethered from patience and wisdom, becomes tyrannical and attempts to force the sufferer out of their sorrow against their will. Such impatient compassion attempts to seize the wheel of the sufferer's emotional vehicle.

In the present case, the seizing happens the other way. The sufferer demands to steer the emotional car of the one trying to help them. We are happy with either. It matters not which person is exercising the tyranny, so long as there is, in the end, only one car. What we want to avoid at all costs is a caravan, that fellowship of sufferings in which the hurting, the suffering, and the afflicted are all permanently tethered to the Enemy, and therefore drawn inexorably toward one another and toward the blazing and damnable light that marks his comforting presence.

Excuse me, Mugwort. That last image has left me feeling ill. I think I'd better lie down.

Your affectionate uncle,
Scratchpot

ABOUT THE AUTHOR

Joe Rigney (PhD, University of Chester) serves as Fellow of Theology at New Saint Andrews College. He is a husband, a father of three, and the author of numerous books: *Live Like a Narnian: Christian Discipleship in Lewis's Chronicles* (Eyes & Pen, 2013); *The Things of Earth: Treasuring God by Enjoying His Gifts* (Canon, 2024); *Lewis on the Christian Life: Becoming Truly Human in the Presence of God* (Crossway, 2018); *Strangely Bright: Can You Love God and Enjoy This World?* (Canon, 2024); *More Than a Battle: Experiencing Victory, Freedom, and Healing from Lust* (B&H, 2021), *Courage: How the Gospel Creates Christian Fortitude* (Crossway, 2023); and *Leadership and Emotional Sabotage: Resisting the Anxiety That Will Wreck Your Family, Destroy Your Church, and Ruin the World* (Canon, 2024). Previously, Dr. Rigney served as a professor at and president of Bethlehem College & Seminary in Minneapolis, a pastor at Cities Church in St. Paul, and a teacher at Desiring God.